Parliaments and the Economic Governance of the European Union

This book analyzes how national parliaments and parliamentary parties performed their legislative, representative and control functions during the reform of European economic governance. Focussing on domestic approvals of anti-crisis measures (EFSF, ESM and the Fiscal Compact) in all member states of the eurozone, the book aims at establishing to what extent national parliaments and parliamentary parties secured their competences in EU policy-making during that process.

This book employs an interdisciplinary approach and analyzes (1) in which states parliaments' formal powers in approval of anti-crisis measures were constrained, (2) how parliamentary parties voted on the analyzed measures, (3) what were the dominant discourses of their proponents and opponents and (4) which parties advocated neoliberal and which Keynesian measures.

This text will be of key interest to scholars, students and practitioners in European Union politics and studies, political parties and parliaments, European Economic governance and more broadly to European politics.

Aleksandra Maatsch is Chair of European and Multilevel Politics (Interim), University of Cologne, Germany.

Routledge Studies on Government and the European Union
Edited by Andy Smith, University of Bordeaux, France

1 **The European Council and European Governance**
   The commanding heights of the EU
   Edited by François Foret and Yann-Sven Rittelmeyer

2 **The EU's Government of Industries**
   Markets, institutions and politics
   Edited by Andy Smith and Bernard Jullien

3 **Policy change in the Area of Freedom, Security and Justice**
   How EU institutions matter
   Edited by Florian Trauner and Ariadna Ripoll Servent

4 **The Mechanisms of Institutional Conflict in the European Union**
   Ludvig Norman

5 **Public Ethics at the European Commission**
   Politics, reform and individual views
   Andreea Năstase

6 **Parliaments and the Economic Governance of the European Union**
   Talking shops or deliberative bodies?
   Aleksandra Maatsch

7 **EU Presidencies between Politics and Administration**
   The governmentality of the Polish, Danish and Cypriot Trio Presidency in 2011–2012
   Mads Dagnis Jensen and Peter Nedergaard

Parliaments and the Economic Governance of the European Union

Talking Shops or Deliberative Bodies?

Aleksandra Maatsch

LONDON AND NEW YORK

First published 2017 by Routledge

2 Park Square, Milton Park, Abingdon, Oxfordshire OX14 4RN
711 Third Avenue, New York, NY 10017

Routledge is an imprint of the Taylor & Francis Group, an informa business

First issued in paperback 2018

Copyright © 2017 Aleksandra Maatsch

The right of Aleksandra Maatsch to be identified as author of this work has been asserted by her in accordance with sections 77 and 78 of the Copyright, Designs and Patents Act 1988.

All rights reserved. No part of this book may be reprinted or reproduced or utilized in any form or by any electronic, mechanical, or other means, now known or hereafter invented, including photocopying and recording, or in any information storage or retrieval system, without permission in writing from the publishers.

Notice:
Product or corporate names may be trademarks or registered trademarks, and are used only for identification and explanation without intent to infringe.

British Library Cataloguing in Publication Data
A catalogue record for this book is available from the British Library

Library of Congress Cataloging-in-Publication Data
Names: Maatsch, Aleksandra, 1979– author.
Title: Parliaments and the economic governance of the European Union : talking shops or deliberative bodies? / Aleksandra Maatsch.
Description: New York : Routledge, 2017. | Series: Routledge studies on government and the European Union | Includes bibliographical references and index.
Identifiers: LCCN 2016029226 | ISBN 9781138230033 (hardback) | ISBN 9781315387260 (ebook)
Subjects: LCSH: European Union countries—Social conditions—21st century. | Central-local government relations—European Union countries. | Decentralization in government—Law and legislation—European Union countries. | European Union countries—Economic policy.
Classification: LCC HN373.5 .M33 2017 | DDC 306.0947—dc23
LC record available at https://lccn.loc.gov/2016029226

ISBN: 978-1-138-23003-3 (hbk)
ISBN: 978-1-138-32644-6 (pbk)

Typeset in Times New Roman
by Apex CoVantage, LLC

Contents

List of tables viii
Preface ix

1 Introduction 1

*National parliaments in the reform of European economic
governance: talking shops or deliberative bodies? 1
National parliaments in the European Union: from
de-parliamentarization to re-parliamentarization 4
The role of parliaments in the European Union after
the Lisbon Treaty 8
How do parliaments contribute to closing
the legitimacy gap? 11
Contents of the book 14*

**2 European financial crisis: dominant narratives
and the legal status of anti-crisis measures** 22

*The European financial crisis 22
The legal status of anti-crisis measures 30
Conclusions 33*

**3 Empowered or disempowered? The role of national
parliaments during the reform of European economic
governance** 36

*Introduction 36
The database 37*

The role of parliamentary oversight in European
   policy-making 42
Emergency legislation: conceptualization 45
Application of emergency legislation during the European
   financial crisis – empirical evidence 46
What factors influenced the application of emergency
   legislation during the reform of European economic
   governance? 49
Conclusions 53

4 **Drivers of political parties' voting behaviour in European economic governance: the ultimate decline of the economic cleavage?** 56

Introduction 56
What factors explain political parties' voting patterns on
   European anti-crisis measures? Literature review and
   hypotheses 59
Research design, methodological approach and the
   database used in this study 63
Empirical findings 66
Discussion and conclusions 68

5 **Parliamentary parties' discourses on anti-crisis measures: between solidarity and particularistic interest** 74

Introduction 74
Analytical framework 76
Methodological approach – frame analysis 77
Discursive support and opposition: dominant patterns 78
Pragmatic and idealistic supporters 80
Opponents: nationalists and anti-austerians 82
Conclusions 85

6 **Macroeconomic preferences of national parliamentary parties** 89

Introduction 89
Keynesianism and neoliberalism 91
Which factors account for political parties' positioning on
   macroeconomic policies? Hypotheses of this study 92

Methodological approach of this study 96
   Methodological approach, step one: discourse
     analysis of plenary parliamentary debates 96
   Methodological approach, step two: QCA crisp-set
     analysis 99
Empirical evidence 101
   Positioned parties: evidence from the crisp-set
     QCA analysis 101
   Parties with 'double' positioning and the 'salient'
     ones 103
   Interpretation of the results 104
Conclusions 106

7 Conclusions 108

Approval of anti-crisis measures 109
Control and representative functions 111
Talking shop or deliberative body? 115
Future challenge: national parliaments within the
   European semester 117

References 121
Index 129

Tables

3.1	Approvals of anti-crisis measures	38
4.1	Explanatory factors, party vote outcome on European anti-crisis measures	67
4.2	Regression models on vote outcomes	71
5.1	Dominant frames	79
6.1	Explanation of codes used in the QCA model	95
6.2	Truth table, presence of the outcome (Keynesian positioning)	101
6.3	Complex solution: presence of the outcome (Keynesian positioning)	102
6.4	Truth table: absence of the outcome (neoliberal positioning)	103
6.5	Complex solution: absence of the outcome (neoliberal positioning)	103

Preface

The idea to pursue a book project dealing with the role of national parliaments and parliamentary parties in the reform of European economic governance was born in Madrid in late 2011. During that period I worked as a postdoctoral researcher in the Institute for Public Goods and Policies at the Spanish National Research Council (CSIC). The initial phase of my work consisted of developing the research design and finding proper methodological tools to analyze the diverse datasets, and I profited here enormously from the interdisciplinary composition of Carlos Closa's research group of which I was a member. As a result, this book combines legal analysis of various formal approval procedures of anti-crisis measures with comparative analysis of parliamentary parties' voting behaviour and plenary debates' analysis. The book's methodology combines statistical analysis of vote outcomes with the Qualitative Comparative Analysis (QCA) of parties' macroeconomic preferences as well as comparative discourse analysis. The application of this interdisciplinary multi-method approach would not have been possible without the stimulating discussions I had, usually over *media mañana*, with Cristina Daniela Vintila, Patricio Galella, Pablo Castillo Ortíz and Maria Cecilia Güemes. Thanks to the legal expertise and linguistic support of Patricio Galella, but also Athena Charalamboglou, I was able to incorporate all member states of the eurozone into the empirical analysis. Finally, I would like to express my special gratitude to Carlos Closa for his support and engagement going far beyond this book project.

From autumn 2013, I continued working on the book at the University of Cambridge's Department of Politics and International Studies. The Cambridge-based OPAL (Observatory of Parliaments after the Lisbon Treaty) project team, directed by Julie Smith, was composed of Geoffrey Edwards, Ian Cooper, Ariella Huff and Anna Dzieszkowska. Our cooperation within the OPAL project has had a very stimulating effect on my work on the book project.

The book was finalized in 2015 at the Max Planck Institute for the Study of Societies in Cologne. The research-oriented and very friendly atmosphere

x *Preface*

at the Institute created a unique environment facilitating work-efficiency. I am particularly indebted to Martin Höpner for his very insightful comments and suggestions on selected parts of the book. I would also like to thank the editorial unit at the Institute for their very thorough work.

Most chapters of this book have been presented during various conferences and workshops, predominantly within the framework of the OPAL project and the PADEMIA network (Parliamentary Democracy in Europe). I would like to thank each and every colleague affiliated with the two projects for commenting and discussing my work.

Cologne, August 2015

1 Introduction

National parliaments in the reform of European economic governance: talking shops or deliberative bodies?

Parliament is a deliberative assembly. . . . government and legislation are matters of reason and judgment, and not of inclination; and what sort of reason is that, in which the determination precedes the discussion; in which one set of men deliberate, and another decide; and where those who form the conclusion are perhaps three hundred miles distant from those who hear the arguments? To deliver an opinion, is the right of all men . . . But authoritative instructions . . . which the member is bound blindly and implicitly to obey, to vote, and to argue for, though contrary to the clearest conviction of his judgment and conscience – these are things utterly unknown to the laws of this land, and which arise from a fundamental mistake of the whole order and tenor of our constitution.

(Burke, 1774: 446–448)

Edmund Burke's 'Speech to the Electors of Bristol' reads as a contemporary opinion picturing the weakness of democratic control in European economic governance. Indeed, in the eurozone, *those who deliberate* became decoupled from *those who decide*, decision-making has not been preceded by deliberation and decision-makers' autonomy has been constrained by external pressures. As a consequence, it has been widely acknowledged that the intergovernmental nature of economic reforms has deeply eroded the principle of representative democracy in the European Union (EU; Crum, 2013; Rittberger, 2014).

The reform process of European economic governance constrained the role of national parliaments and the European Parliament. In particular, the ordinary legislative procedure has not been used in the approval of most anti-crisis measures. Governments, under pressure of time, have frequently

2 Introduction

opted to ratify anti-crisis measures with fast-track procedures that accelerated the legislative process but severely limited national parliaments' role. As a consequence, the marginalization of parliaments in the process of reforming European economic governance called into question the Lisbon process that is supposed to promote stronger involvement of parliaments in European policy-making.

This book analyzes how national parliaments contribute to European economic governance. By the same token, the book speaks to the broader literature focussing on the government and the European Union (Foret and Rittelmeyer, 2015; Jullien and Smith, 2016; Norman, 2016). Recent studies analyzing how the EU is actually governed have rightly observed that the government of the EU is not exclusively composed of either national or supranational actors. Rather, European public policies are shaped by different political, technocratic or private actors. The variety of actors involved in tailoring European public policies poses a profound challenge to the legitimacy of decision-making in the EU. This book addresses these concerns by investigating the contribution of national representative institutions to the reform process of European economic governance.

This book is also a contribution to the lively debate on the impact of the European financial crisis on national parliaments' oversight powers. It focusses on national parliaments with a view to providing a comprehensive account of their role in the reform process of the Economic and Monetary Union (EMU). In the contemporary literature we find two contrasting opinions. According to the first, national parliaments have become a 'talking shop', institutions in which discussion is all that happens – neither decisions nor actions arise from such debates. In light of that opinion, national parliaments have become de facto devoid of power to tailor institutional reforms. According to the second position, it is premature to herald the disempowerment of national parliaments because their major task in European policy-making is to control rather than to legislate. In particular, national parliaments are first and foremost supposed to scrutinize their governments' actions at the EU level and to domesticate EU policy-making by bringing it closer to national constituencies.

While the first position evaluates national parliaments' performance from the perspective of their law-making competences, the second focusses on representation and scrutiny. Furthermore, while the first position does not assign any significant importance to deliberation, the second recognizes it as central to the fulfilment of representative and supervisory functions. As a consequence, our evaluation of national parliaments' role in European economic governance – but also in EU policy-making in general – depends on which functions of national parliaments are prioritized.

This book examines national parliaments' performance in the reform of European economic governance without discriminating between the three parliamentary functions. The empirical analysis is guided by the following question: how have national parliaments and, more specifically, parliamentary parties performed their representative, scrutiny and law-making functions during the process of reforming European economic governance?

The empirical analysis presented in this book concerns the period of the institutional reform of European economic governance from 2008 to 2012. The analysis covers all member states of the eurozone. The analysis was conducted at the level of national parliaments and national parliamentary parties; hence, there is not one theoretical framework but two. This is because hypotheses that help to explain phenomena at the level of parliaments are not applicable at the level of parliamentary parties. However, only an approach combining the two levels of analysis can help us to establish retrospectively what role national parliaments have performed during the reform of European economic governance. As a result, each chapter of the book can be read separately.

The book investigates the following aspects of national parliaments' involvement in the reform of European economic governance: (1) Were national parliaments *formally* empowered or disempowered? What procedures were adopted at the national level in order to approve subsequent anti-crisis measures (EFSF, ESM, Fiscal Compact)? Were anti-crisis measures adopted with fast-track procedures – limiting parliaments' involvement – or standard procedures? Have national supreme and constitutional courts empowered or disempowered particular national parliaments with their rulings? (2) Which national parliamentary parties voted in favour and which voted against the analyzed anti-crisis measures? (3) What were the dominant arguments of supporters and opponents of particular anti-crisis measures? How can we explain the differences in supporters' and opponents' arguments? (4) What were the macroeconomic preferences of national parliamentary parties? In particular, which parties advocated neoliberal policies and which were in favour of Keynesian ones?

By focussing on representative institutions, namely, parliamentary parties and national parliaments, the book does not investigate the individual dimension. In particular, the book does not analyze how individual members of the parliament engaged with the financial crisis. This is not to say that the individual dimension is less important: on the contrary, the internal dynamic within each political party is crucial for its voting behaviour and positions on most important policies. However, the analysis of internal party dynamics requires an in-depth, case-oriented approach. This book, on the contrary, aims at establishing the dominant patterns at the level of the whole eurozone.

4 *Introduction*

Finally, this book employs a broad variety of research methods. In particular, Chapter 3 draws on comparative legal analysis. Chapter 4 presents a statistical analysis of parliamentary parties' votes on anti-crisis measures (binary logit model). Chapter 5 employs comparative qualitative discourse analysis in order to analyze which arguments were voiced by supporters and opponents of particular anti-crisis measures. Finally, Chapter 6, investigating the macroeconomic preferences of parliamentary parties, combines qualitative comparative discourse analysis with the Qualitative Comparative Analysis (QCA) developed by Charles Ragin.

National parliaments in the European Union: from de-parliamentarization to re-parliamentarization

National parliaments and the European Parliament could not have reacted in a more different way to the process of European integration. In particular, whereas the European Parliament has always claimed a maximum interpretation of its competences, national parliaments accepted the limitation of their law-making and control powers by ratifying subsequent European treaties. Interestingly, until the 1990s national parliaments have not perceived the increase of the Council's and the Commission's power as a direct threat to their constitutive competences. National parliaments rather believed that the EU does not intervene in their areas of activity. Furthermore, they chose not to become involved with European matters as these were not perceived as vote-seeking issues; after all, until the 1900s European matters were recognized as policies without politics (Schmidt, 2011). As a result, in the first decades of the European integration process national parliaments were not motivated to develop expertise – or administrative support structures – in European issues.

However, with the deepening of the European integration process, national parliaments realized that both their law-making and control powers became reduced. In particular, not only the number of directives increased over time but also their scope. Furthermore, exercise of control functions became increasingly difficult for national parliaments because the Qualified Majority Vote (QMV) was extended to new policy areas. It has been observed that the two institutional developments generated a dual democratic deficit (Judge, 1995). First, national parliaments were affected by the transfer of authority to the EU level and, second, they could no longer make their governments act according to their preferences.

In the 1990s the process of de-parliamentarization in the EU was interrupted (Maatsch, 2013). On one hand, national parliaments began to adapt incrementally to the new circumstances and engage with EU politics (Maurer and Wessels, 2001). Norton (1995) identified three phases of national parliaments' adaptation to the European integration. During the first phase (from the 1950s to late 1980s) the involvement of national parliaments with EU matters was minimal. During the second phase (from the mid-1980s to the entry into force of the Treaty of Maastricht in 1993) the scope of EU-related policies increased significantly. As a result, most national parliaments established committees for European integration. Before, European matters usually remained within the responsibility of committees for International Affairs. During that phase national parliaments began to engage systematically with European matters. Finally, during the third phase (from 1993 onwards) the role of national parliaments in EU affairs became recognized for the first time in the treaties. In particular, in the Treaty of Maastricht (1993) the EU member states made a declaration on greater involvement of national parliaments in the activities of the EU. Furthermore, there was also a declaration on a Conference of Parliaments which established new forms of reporting by the Council and the Commission. The Amsterdam Treaty (1999) included a protocol on the role of national parliaments which became incorporated into the main body of the Treaty. The Treaty has also fostered national parliaments' access to the Commission's documents. The second element of the protocol concerned the establishment of the Conference of Parliamentary Committees for Union Affairs (COSAC). Furthermore, beginning from the 1990s, political decision-makers became more concerned with the representative character of the European Union and, by the same token, envisaged more pronounced role for the European and national parliaments.

The Treaty of Lisbon constitutes by now the most significant step towards recognition of parliaments' role in the European Union. Foremost, it emphasized the role of national parliaments and the European Parliament in closing the legitimacy gap in EU politics. The reform comprised fostering the supervisory function of national parliaments and the law-making function of the European Parliament. Extension of the European Parliament's law-making competences, by means of co-decision and then the ordinary legislative procedure, has fostered the legitimacy of European decision-making. The ordinary legislative procedure guarantees that European legislation is scrutinized and approved (or disapproved) by directly elected representatives of European citizens (and not exclusively by the Council). The Lisbon Treaty has also fostered the control function of national parliaments through control-related activities (scrutiny reserve, Early Warning Mechanism), as well as vertical and horizontal exchange of information between national parliaments and the European Parliament.

Finally, the Lisbon process has also brought about new transnational developments. The Conference of Parliamentary Committees for Union Affairs (COSAC) established a permanent secretariat that helps to produce reports on parliamentary scrutiny. In order to improve access to information concerning the legislative process, a website IPEX has been established. Furthermore, two interparliamentary conferences have been established: the Interparliamentary Conference for the Common Foreign and Security Policy and the Common Security and Defence Policy as well as the Interparliamentary Conference on Economic and Financial Governance.

Although the institutional change introduced with the Lisbon Treaty has helped to reduce the legitimacy gap in the European Union, it has by no means been able to eliminate it. This is because, first, the scope of the reform was limited. National parliaments' control powers were extended only in issues related to subsidiarity. Second, *internal* institutional limitations generated other obstacles. Namely, it has been observed that not all national parliaments have equally generous democratic arrangements (De Witte et al, 2010). In Europe, practices regarding parliamentary control in general are very diverse. While in some states national legislation equips parliaments with strong supervisory powers, in other states legislators' powers can be minimal (Fasone, 2014b). Recent comparative study demonstrates (Hefftler et al., 2015) that the adaptation process towards the EU integration contributed to the emergence of different ideal–typical forms of national parliaments' involvement. Analyzing all national parliaments of the European Union, the study identified the following types of parliaments: policy-shapers (proactive, often equipped with mandating rights), governments' watchdogs, public forum (actively communicating with voters), EU expert and European player (active directly at the EU level). As a result, we can conclude that national parliaments adapted to the European integration process; however, their institutional responses are far from being unanimous. Furthermore, there is also variation in non-formal practices, for instance, regarding the amount and quality of administrative support (Auel and Christiansen, 2015). As a consequence, not all national parliaments can scrutinize EU policies equally well.

Against that background, there is no agreement in the literature on how to assess national parliaments' adaptation to the of European integration process. One group of scholars claims that de-parliamentarization is, in fact, a permanent trend (e.g. Weiler, 1999; Maurer and Wessels, 2001; Kaczynski, 2011). These scholars draw their inference from the comparative analysis of institutional formal powers. It has to be admitted that formal law-making, control and representation powers of national parliaments were constrained due to the European integration process. At the same time, domestic and European executive institutions (governments and the Council) experienced an increase of power. Despite various institutional reforms, the dominance of the executive has still not been counter-balanced.

Introduction 7

At the same time, there are also studies demonstrating that the analysis of formal powers is not sufficient to account for the role of national parliaments in the European Union. As Auel observed (2007: 53), 'Effectiveness of parliamentary influence cannot simply be measured by looking at formal parliamentary participation right, but needs to take into account whether and how these formal capabilities translate into parliamentary behaviour.' According to these studies, national parliaments experienced a period of disempowerment, but eventually they managed to adapt to the new circumstances (Judge, 1995; Bergman, 1997; Raunio and Hix, 2000; Auel and Benz, 2005; O'Brennen and Raunio, 2007). For instance, it has been demonstrated that due to the European integration process national parliaments became active in new policy areas (Duina and Oliver, 2005). Furthermore, the EU fostered interparliamentary processes of communication, knowledge exchange and data-sharing. However, national parliaments are not always interested to engage equally in all EU issues. In fact, the literature demonstrated that national parliaments are deliberately very selective in their approach; hence, sometimes they are interested to delegate or abdicate some powers (Saalfeld, 2005; De Ruiter, 2013). From that perspective, weaker activity or influence in a given policy area is not always something that *happens* to national parliaments; rather, it can be a deliberately made decision, for instance, if the issue in question lacks domestic salience or it cannot be incorporated into the dominant domestic cleavages (De Ruiter, 2013).

Finally, given the fact that national parliaments' major role in the EU is to control their governments and to domesticate EU issues at the national level (Bellamy and Kröger, 2016), their influence does not exclusively depend on the strength of formal powers but rather on their *willingness* to conduct oversight of European issues. According to the classical – by now – typology of Born and Hänggi (2004, 2005), parliamentary oversight depends on three factors: authority (formal competences), ability (administrative resources) and attitude (willingness to perform oversight). The authors claimed that while formal powers constitute a central factor, abilities and attitudes of parliamentarians can effectively modify oversight practices. For instance, there are studies illustrating that the existence of formal powers is not necessary for parliaments in order to conduct oversight. When MPs have strong incentives to engage in oversight, they can do so – by means of written questions or reports – despite the lack of strong formal powers. On the contrary, if formal powers are not accompanied by a certain grade of domestic politicization, parliaments are likely to limit their oversight to mandatory procedures (Galella and Maatsch, 2016). As a result, the existing literature suggests that a proper assessment of national parliaments' activity in the European Union always has to take into consideration the three factors accounting for parliamentary oversight activity, namely: formal legal powers, administrative support and the willingness to exercise oversight.

The role of parliaments in the European Union after the Lisbon Treaty

Article 10 of the Treaty on European Union (TEU) introduced explicit references to democratic principles aimed at reinforcing the representative and participatory dimensions of democracy in the European Union. In particular, in order to improve representation, the Treaty extended the European Parliament's legislative competences and strengthened national parliaments' supervisory powers. It has been observed that

> National parliaments were not randomly picked for the job. Instead, they were selected in the hope that their review will provide legitimacy to a European political project that faces an increasing gap between a small Europeanised and Europhoric elite, and less convinced European citizens. Thus, national parliaments are perceived as an unexploited reservoir of legitimacy that the Union can use to counter the democratic deficit.
>
> (De Witte et al., 2010: 22)

Finally, the participatory dimension has been fostered through the introduction of new mechanisms, such as the European citizens' initiative (Mayoral, 2011).

In general, national parliaments perform different functions in EU and in national politics. While in domestic politics national parliaments enjoy the right to propose, amend, pass or reject bills, at the European level their impact is far more restricted. The Treaty explicitly confirms that the major functions of national parliaments in the European Union consist of, first, establishing a channel of accountability between the Council and national constituencies and, second, scrutinizing the decision-making process at the EU level.

Article 10 TEU stipulates that 'Member States are represented in the European Council by their Heads of State or Government and in the Council by their governments, themselves democratically accountable either to their national Parliaments, or to their citizens.' Furthermore, Article 12 reads that 'National Parliaments contribute actively to the good functioning of the Union.' Article 12 identifies six areas in which national parliaments make a contribution.

First, national parliaments are informed about the progress of the legislative process at the EU level. The Treaty provides that all documents of the European Commission be transmitted directly to national parliaments.

Details concerning the process are stipulated in Title 1 of Protocol No. 1 on the Role of National Parliaments in the European Union, Articles 1–8.

Second, in Article 12(b) TEU national parliaments are recognized as guardians of the subsidiarity principle (details are stipulated in Protocol No. 2 on the Application of the Principles of Subsidiarity and Proportionality). The so-called Early Warning System envisages that national parliaments issue 'yellow' or 'orange' cards: a yellow card can be submitted to the Commission within eight weeks[1] if it is supported by one third of the votes assigned to legislatures.[2] The Commission then decides whether to maintain, amend or withdraw a given proposal and justifies its position in a written response to parliaments. The orange card can be waived if a simple majority of national parliaments sends an opinion on an infringement of the subsidiarity principle within eight weeks. If the Commission wishes to uphold a proposal that has been contested by a simple majority of national parliaments, it has to present its opinion to the European Parliament and the Council. If 55 percent of the Council and a simple majority in the European Parliament conclude that a given proposal violates the principle of subsidiarity, the proposal is withheld from the legislative process.

Third, national parliaments have been recognized as contributing to the good functioning of the Union through monitoring of the area of security and justice.

The fourth, fifth and sixth functions are: taking part in the revision procedures of the Treaties, being notified of applications for accession to the EU and participating in interparliamentary cooperation between national parliaments and the European Parliament (details are laid down in the above-mentioned Protocol, Title II on Inter-parliamentary Cooperation, Articles 9 and 10). In particular, parliamentary participation in Treaty revisions has been confirmed within the ordinary legislative procedure. In light of the Passerelle clause, when the European Council decides to extend qualified majority voting to a new policy area or to shift from a special legislative procedure to co-decision, national parliaments are entitled to veto this decision. Finally, Protocol No. 1 also constitutes the legal basis for the creation of new bodies for interparliamentary cooperation, aimed at stimulating national parliaments' horizontal exchange of ideas and information, but providing no legislative competences. In 2012 an Interparliamentary Conference for the Common Foreign and Security Policy was established to replace the Assembly of the Western European Union. In 2013, under provisions of Article 13 of the Fiscal Compact, an Interparliamentary Conference on Economic and Financial Governance came into existence (Cooper, 2014).

Furthermore, international trade became an exclusive competence of the European Union, which means that the European Parliament replaced national legislators in scrutinizing free trade agreements (Article 219 Treaty on the Functioning of the European Union [TFEU]). National parliaments are entitled to participate in the ratification process only if the free trade agreement in question is recognized as a 'mixed agreement', namely, one that contains issues in which the EU does not have exclusive competence. Also, the European Parliament acquired stronger control over proposals emerging from committees. The TFEU created a new category of legal acts – namely, delegated acts – whose general aim is to accelerate the legislative process. Under certain circumstances, when an amendment of an existing act concerns non-essential elements, the European Parliament and the Council have the option of seceding their powers to the Commission, which adopts the amendment. According to the TFEU, the Council and the European Parliament stipulate the scope and duration of delegation in each case. With TFEU the European Parliament also acquired powers in the monitoring of implementing acts. That is, if a certain law requires uniform implementation in all EU member states, the Commission is entitled to issue an act stipulating the exact terms of the implementation process (Article 291 TFEU). With TFEU the European Parliament acquired powers (by means of ordinary legislative procedure) to authorize the Commission to adopt implementing acts. Prior to the TFEU, the authorization remained exclusively within the competences of the Council.

The European Parliament also acquired limited powers to propose legislation. According to Article 225 TFEU the European Parliament is entitled to address the Commission and ask for a legislative proposal on a given matter. If the Commission chooses not to issue a legislative proposal, it has to notify the Parliament. In the same vein, the European Parliament became entitled to present the Council with proposals for treaty amendments, both through the ordinary revision procedure and the simplified procedure. Finally, the European Parliament has also become entitled to elect – upon a proposal by the European Council – the President of the Commission and to approve the High Representative of the Union for Foreign Affairs and Security Policy. Together with national parliaments, the European Parliament acquired new competences to control the area of freedom, security and justice, as well as the European External Action Service (Article 27(3) TFEU). The TFEU further extended the European Parliament's powers regarding the adoption of flexibility clauses. According to Article 352 TFEU the use of flexibility clauses is subject to the special legislative procedure. The European Parliament has also acquired powers in the procedure regulating withdrawal of a member state from the European Union. In particular, the Council is entitled to decide on a withdrawal once it has been approved by the European Parliament.

The extension of the European Parliament's legislative competences in EU policies has clearly contributed to the democratization of decision-making in the European Union. This is because the European Parliament, as a directly elected European institution, enjoys direct input legitimacy. The reform has also confirmed the basic division of competences between the European Parliament and national legislators in EU policies: accordingly, while the primary function of the European Parliament is to *legislate*, the responsibility of national parliaments is to *scrutinize*.

Already in the symbolic dimension the Treaty stressed the fact that the European Parliament constitutes a *direct* channel of representation for *EU citizens*. Under the Nice Treaty, MEPs were recognized as representatives of the peoples of the *States* brought together in the Community (Article 189 Treaty Establishing the European Community [TEC]). In contrast, according to Article 14.2 TEU, members of the European Parliament are representatives of the *Union's citizens*.[3] The TEU has also introduced changes to the composition of the European Parliament by increasing the number of MEPs from 736 to 751 (750 plus the President). The rules for allocating seats are (digressively) proportional to the population of each state. Furthermore, the TEU stipulates that while the maximum number of seats assigned to a member state is 96, the minimum is 6 seats.

The Treaty has empowered the European Parliament primarily through the extension of co-decision (now the ordinary legislative procedure) to new policy areas. As has been noted in the literature, the main novelty is not the establishment of rules of procedure but rather the extension of the European Parliament's legislative powers to new policy areas (De Witte et al., 2010). The existing co-decision procedure – renamed the ordinary legislative procedure – has been extended to cover approximately 90 percent of EU legislation (De Witte et al., 2010). The areas covered by the ordinary legislative procedure are: agriculture and fisheries, common commercial policy and, with a few exceptions, police and criminal justice.

How do parliaments contribute to closing the legitimacy gap?

The literature differentiates between input (accountability) and output legitimacy (Scharpf, 2009). Whereas output legitimacy concerns the performance of institutions in delivering outcomes, input legitimacy denotes conditions for democratic self-government and the electoral accountability of governors. In short, in democratic self-governing polities, power is delegated to decision-makers (the executive) whose performance is constantly evaluated by directly elected representatives (members of the national parliament). In order to remain well-informed, parliamentary parties scrutinize governments, among other things, by means of hearings or question hours. Apart from that, MPs are entitled to make formal suggestions to their governments by means of motions, resolutions or even – in some cases – laws. Furthermore, if parliamentarians come to the conclusion that their government is failing to perform its functions, they can raise a motion of no-confidence against a particular minister or the whole cabinet. In sum, the conditions for input legitimacy are fulfilled if a national parliament scrutinizes a government's proceedings and has powers to hold it accountable for its actions.

Voters constitute the third actor in the 'accountability chain': they elect representatives (members of the national parliament) in the national general elections and, after elections, they follow and scrutinize the political performance of their representatives. Finally, if voters are not satisfied with the work of elected representatives, they can manifest their dissatisfaction by voting for a different party in the next elections. The institution that helps voters to follow and evaluate the performance of their elected representatives is the media.

At the EU level, replication of the national accountability chain is problematic. The European integration process, understood as centralization of decision-making at the EU level, has contributed to decreasing input legitimacy. With European integration, more and more decisions that were previously within the competences of national legislators have been delegated to the European level. In the course of that process, national parliaments have been disempowered in the exercise of their two core domains in EU politics: law-making and executive scrutiny. As a consequence, the role of national parliaments in EU politics has become, with exception of EU treaty ratifications or revisions, limited to transposing EU directives into national legislation. The extension of Qualitative Majority Voting (QMV) to new policy areas has also further diminished the role of national parliaments in EU politics. In particular, under QMV there is no guarantee that a final Council decision corresponds to the initial government position approved by the national parliament.[4] Beyond institutional factors, parliamentary administrators often claim to be overwhelmed by the complexity of European issues. MPs themselves are frequently uncertain about the extent to which their national mandate entitles them to engage in European policy-making. As a consequence of these developments national parliaments have been widely recognized as the greatest 'losers' with regard to European integration (Maurer and Wessels, 2001; O'Brennan and Raunio, 2007).

Nor is the European Parliament free from internal institutional limitations. Although the European Parliament is directly elected, European party groups are not directly accountable to national constituencies (Borz and Rose, 2013). Rather, national parties compete for seats in the European Parliament domestically and, in the next step, they establish or enter an already existing European party group. As a consequence, it is easier for ideologically homogenous party groups to fulfil their electoral promises because their transnational constituencies share similar preferences and values. By contrast, in ideologically heterogeneous party groups, the likelihood of internal conflicts among constitutive national parties is much higher (Borz and Rose, 2013).

The European financial crisis distorted the institutional process oriented towards minimizing the legitimacy gap in the European Union. In particular, during the reform of European economic governance, the involvement of the European Parliament and national parliaments in the decision-making processes was very limited. As a consequence, it has been widely observed that the intergovernmental nature of the economic reforms deeply eroded the principle of representative democracy (Crum, 2013; Rittberger, 2014). Parliaments were hardly represented in that process: the European Parliament was basically excluded, while national parliaments played only a consultative role (Fasone, 2014a).

During the European financial crisis the quality of input and output legitimacy decreased. Although input legitimacy was already deficient before the crisis, the defects were experienced profoundly by citizens when decision-makers failed to meet the requirements of output legitimacy (Scharpf, 2014). In other words, voters in bailout states realized that they have very little means at their disposal to influence contested decisions. That was mainly because the drafters of budgetary measures enshrined in rescue packages (including Memorandums of Understanding, loan agreements and their revisions) – namely, the European Commission, the European Central Bank and the International Monetary Fund (the 'Troika') – are not accountable to voters in the bailout states. As Mair observed, governments in bailout states were, therefore, no longer recognized by their voters as 'governments by the people' but rather 'governments against the people' (2011: 6).

Recent contributions to the debate on the institutional order of European economic governance have widely acknowledged that neither a fully-fledged federalization of the EU (a 'transfer union') nor dissolution of the EMU is politically realistic. For that reason most proposals aim at improving the existing institutional order by decentralizing executive-based decision-making and control. It has been proposed to apply the ordinary legislative procedure to all future legislative changes within the European economic governance, as well as to grant national parliaments a stronger role in controlling decision-making (Crum, 2013; Kröger and Bellamy, 2016).

The concept of 'republican intergovernmentalism' (Kröger and Bellamy, 2016) draws on the assumption that national parliaments could reconnect the European integration process with the communal self-rule of the EU member states. Active involvement of national parliaments in the reform process could also contribute to addressing the depoliticization of EU policy-making by 'domesticating' and 'normalizing' it. Normalization of EU politics would involve national parliaments reconnecting EU politics to the left–right economic cleavage. In light of that proposal, the democratic deficit on the input side would be alleviated by re-establishing the channel of accountability between the European decision-making level, national parliaments and voters. There are also more specific proposals, for example, to institutionalize national parliaments' control in the form of a supranational conference of national parliaments equipped with substantial scrutiny powers (Crum, 2013).

However, all normative proposals advocating the strengthening of parliamentary control should be preceded by a thorough empirical investigation of the institutional conditions under which national parliaments conduct oversight of European economic governance. This is because parliamentary scrutiny is influenced by both domestic and international factors. These institutional developments can have either an empowering or a disempowering effect on parliaments. Furthermore, domestic and international asymmetries can have very different effect depending on where we identify the locus of legitimacy to be. In particular, whereas unilateral empowerment of a national parliament by a constitutional court fosters the supervisory powers of that parliament, it decreases the legitimacy of parliamentary oversight in the EU by deepening asymmetries of power among national parliaments. In the following sections we map the asymmetries and evaluate their impact on input legitimacy in the European Union.

Contents of the book

This book provides a comprehensive account of how national parliaments became involved in the reform of European economic governance. Chapter 1 introduces the major research questions guiding the analysis. The following subchapter outlines the formal competences assigned to national parliaments and the European Parliament by the Lisbon Treaty; it demonstrates that the process of empowering parliaments fostered by the Treaty has been interrupted during the reform of European economic governance. The chapter then discusses shortly how parliaments help to close the input legitimacy gap in the European Union. In the final section, the content of each chapter is presented.

Chapter 2 provides necessary background information, such as explanatory narratives, identifying the causes of the financial crisis and details of the legal status of anti-crisis measures. The chapter begins by enquiring into the *nature* of the European financial crisis; in particular, is it a financial crisis, a banking crisis, a sovereign debt crisis, a crisis of trade imbalances or a mortgage crisis? Furthermore, can we consider the European crisis to be an extension of the global financial crisis or an entirely different phenomenon? The chapter seeks to demonstrate that the European crisis was invoked by a combination of three types of factors: global financial crisis, the institutional weaknesses of EMU and the domestic weaknesses of national economies. In particular, the chapter asserts that Greece constitutes a special, rather than a representative, case, given the causes of the crisis. Whereas in Greece the crisis was triggered by – among other things – fiscal irresponsibility on the part of success governments, in Ireland, Spain, Portugal and Cyprus, the roots of the crisis were rather to be found in banking practices.

Given the institutional weaknesses of EMU, the chapter demonstrates that eurozone has not been exclusively an economic but also a political project (Dyson and Featherstone, 1999; McNamara, 1999). The common currency was introduced even though many economists and political scientists argued that the EU was not an *optimum* currency area (Enderlein and Verdun, 2009; Krugman, 2012). In particular, it has been observed that the eurozone meets only two of the three necessary conditions for establishing a common currency zone. The first – fulfilled – condition is labour mobility among member states; the second – also fulfilled – condition is intensive trade relations among member states. The third condition is fiscal union, but of course that has not yet been met. However, upon the introduction of euro, there was a belief that a full-fledged fiscal union was not necessary because peer pressure would be sufficient to maintain fiscal discipline in accordance with the rules laid down in the Stability and Growth Pact (Townsend, 2006).

The second part of the chapter presents the legal status of the major anti-crisis measures: the European Financial Stability Facility (EFSF) (establishment of the fund and increase of its budgetary capacity), the European Stability Mechanism (ESM) and the Treaty on Stability, Coordination and Governance in the Economic and Monetary Union (TSCG) – also referred to as the 'Fiscal Compact'. Although all the abovementioned measures belong to the so-called 'reform package', their contents differ substantially. The EFSF and the ESM established a bailout fund to provide financial support to eurozone member states that could no longer finance themselves on the markets (due to liquidity or solvency problems). While the EFSF was established as a temporary solution, the ESM became a permanent bailout fund. The Fiscal Compact is a stricter version of the previous Stability and Growth Pact. Member states bound by the treaty are required to introduce into domestic law a self-correcting mechanism that is supposed to ensure that their national budgets balance. In particular, the general budget deficit shall not exceed 3 percent of GDP, the structural deficit shall be less than 1 percent of GDP and the debt-to-GDP ratio shall remain below 60 percent. In general, while the EFSF and the ESM deepened financial solidarity in

European economic governance, the Fiscal Compact strengthened budgetary surveillance.

Chapter 3 investigates how the intergovernmental reform process of European economic governance affected national parliaments' oversight of that policy area. The Lisbon Treaty, heralded as the 'Treaty of parliaments' (Rittberger, 2014), strengthened the law-making competences of the European Parliament, as well as national legislators' supervisory powers in European policy-making. However, European economic governance has been reformed predominantly by means of various intergovernmental measures limiting the role of national legislators and the European Parliament (Dawson and de Witte, 2013). The question emerged: which parliaments became disempowered and which managed to secure their formal powers in that process – and why? The dependent variable of the study is operationalized as the presence or absence of 'emergency legislation' allowing governments to accelerate the legislative process and minimize the risk of a default by constraining national parliaments' powers. This chapter examines how national parliaments in all eurozone states were involved in approving the following measures: the EFSF (establishment and increase of budgetary capacity), the ESM and the Fiscal Compact. The findings demonstrate that whereas northern European parliaments' powers were secured (or in some cases even fostered), southern European parliaments were disempowered due to the following factors: (1) domestic constitutional set-up permitting emergency legislation, (2) national supreme or constitutional courts' consent to extensive application of emergency legislation and (3) international economic and political pressure on governments to prevent default of the legislative process. Due to significant power asymmetries national parliaments remained *de jure* but not *de facto* equal in the exercise of their control powers at the EU level. As a consequence, both the disempowerment of particular parliaments and the asymmetry of powers among them had a negative effect on the legitimacy of European economic governance.

Domestic constitutional set-up permitting emergency legislation has been operationalized as fast-track procedures and mergers. Fast-track procedures are applied in exceptional situations when a given bill has to be approved in a short time. These procedures shorten the legislative process and limit the involvement of national parliaments (for instance, it is common practice in many states to accelerate the approval process by limiting the number of parliamentary readings from three to one). Mergers constitute legal packages comprising two or more bills submitted to national parliament for discussion and vote. Parliaments have only one vote in order to approve or reject the whole legal package. Finally, national supreme or constitutional courts can confirm national parliaments' powers in their rulings; however, courts can also use their competences in order to disempower parliaments.

Introduction 17

In sum, most supreme or constitutional courts in the eurozone have not assumed an active role of parliaments' defenders. Particularly the position of southern European courts has contributed to diminishing the role of national parliaments in states that were most directly affected by the new legislative measures. However, the most prominent example of national parliaments' empowerment can be found in Germany.[5] In the first ruling on the EFSF and the Economic Adjustment Programme for Greece of 9 July 2011, the German Constitutional Court declared that neither international treaty violates the Basic Law. However, it also stressed that the Bundestag cannot transfer its budgetary powers to other actors. In these respects, the Court's ruling precluded the approval of anti-crisis measures by means of special fast-track procedures that exclude national legislators. The second ruling – of 2 August 2012 – precluded the possibility of delegating powers belonging to the whole parliamentary plenum to a special parliamentary committee that is supposed to decide on urgent matters related to European economic governance. In the third ruling on the ESM and the Euro Plus Pact of 6 March 2012, the Court stated that the government is obliged to inform the German parliament as early as possible regarding all matters related to European economic governance. Finally, in the ruling on the ESM and the Fiscal Compact of 9 December 2012, the Court stipulated that the parliament has to be consulted on each increase in the ESM budget and on new bailout decisions.

There is also an international asymmetry with regard to substantive equality standards which concerns the de facto equality of institutions in the exercise of their competences (not formalized legal powers). For instance, the acquisition of bailout loans has also been conditioned on completing ratification of the Fiscal Compact and introducing the balanced budget rule into domestic legislation. That condition has also constrained national parliaments in exercising their powers: practically speaking, parliaments in bailout states could neither reject the Fiscal Compact nor delay the ratification process. Otherwise they risked losing financial aid.

Analysis of the approval processes of all major anti-crisis tools (EFSF, ESM and the Fiscal Compact) in all national parliaments of the eurozone demonstrates that the impact of national parliaments was both *limited* and *asymmetrical*. Parliaments in debtor states were more profoundly affected by domestic and international asymmetries than creditor states. Their supervisory powers were severely limited through fast-track procedures and mergers but also by the lack of substantive equality among national parliaments in the eurozone.

Chapter 4 analyzes the factors that account for parliamentary parties' votes on the EFSF, the ESM and the Fiscal Compact in 16 eurozone states. The chapter tests various explanatory variables in order to establish whether parliamentary parties voted *responsibly* (prioritizing international obligations) or *responsively* (prioritizing voters' preferences). *Responsibility* is defined in this chapter as respect for international obligations towards regional organizations or international markets (Bardi et al., 2014). In the empirical dimension, the chapter tests the extent to which the vote outcome can be explained by the following factors: (1) international interdependence, (2) response to voters' preferences, (3) institutional cleavage (government/opposition), (4) economic policy preferences, (5) parties' positions on the EU, (6) conflicts between creditors and debtors and (7) formal approval procedures. The empirical analysis is conducted with the help of the statistical binary logit model; the unit of the analysis is defined as the vote of a particular party on a given anti-crisis measure.

The empirical findings demonstrate that whereas almost all governing parties supported anti-crisis measures, opposition parties were either in favour of or against them. In the chapter, governing parties' support is explained in terms of their international obligations. Opposition parties' positions reflected their attitude to European integration: Eurosceptic parties tended to vote against. Furthermore, whereas negative votes among opposition parties were less likely the higher the trust of the population in its government and the satisfaction with the EU's problem-solving capacity, the likelihood of a no-vote increased proportionally to the level of trust in national parliaments. Opposition parties' policy preferences measured on the economic left–right scale have not yielded significant results nor has an additional test measuring the impact of extreme left–right positions.

In sum, the results demonstrated that whereas governing parties voted *responsibly* – that is, prioritizing international obligations – opposition parties were more prone to vote *responsively*. The major factor explaining opposition parties' vote outcomes was their position on the EU. In particular, that finding demonstrates that opposition parties' position on anti-crisis measures boiled down to the basic question of whether a given party supported the European integration project or not. As a consequence, Eurosceptic opposition parties opposed anti-crisis measures, whereas pro-EU opposition parties supported them.

Furthermore, opposition parties' vote outcomes have been fairly responsive towards voters' preferences. In particular, in states where voters' trust in their governments was high, opposition parties were more likely to vote in favour of all analyzed anti-crisis measures. By contrast, opposition parties were more prone to vote against anti-crisis measures if voters' trust in national parliaments was high. Finally, the analysis also demonstrated that the higher the public trust in the capacity of the EU to solve the financial crisis, the more likely the opposition parties were to vote in favour of anti-crisis measures.

Chapter 5 presents the results of comparative qualitative discourse analysis of plenary debates accompanying approval of the increased budgetary capacity of the EFSF and the ratification of the Fiscal Compact. The empirical analysis was conducted with help of Atlas.ti software. Discourses were clustered according to the classification of Habermas (1991), who distinguishes between pragmatic, ethical and moral arguments.

The states under study were: Austria, Belgium, France, Germany, Greece, Ireland, Luxembourg, the Netherlands, Slovakia, Slovenia and Spain. Although the analysis does not cover all the member states of the eurozone, the selected cases include both creditor and debtor states. The analysis was also limited to two anti-crisis measures: the increased budgetary capacity of the EFSF and the ratification of the Fiscal Compact. These two measures were representative in the sense that they made it possible to investigate how parliamentary parties position themselves on a bailout fund requiring financial solidarity among member states, as well as the Fiscal Compact, which introduces stricter financial surveillance. This chapter addresses the following questions: what were the major reasons behind support or rejection of anti-crisis measures among national parliamentary parties? How convergent or divergent were parties in their choice of arguments supporting or rejecting anti-crisis measures? How can we explain the discursive differences among parliamentary parties?

The empirical analysis demonstrates that discursive supporters of anti-crisis measures were divided into idealistic and pragmatic ones. Within the group of opponents we could also identify two sub-groups: nationalists and anti-austerians. Pragmatic supporters were composed of governing parties who referred predominantly to particularistic national economic interests. In contrast, idealistic supporters – represented by mainstream opposition parties – more frequently employed ethical arguments referring to the political value of the European Union and the value of the European integration process as such. As a result, the major drivers of institutional reform were pragmatic and ethical discourses.

The discursive opponents of the anti-crisis measures under analysis employed two very different types of discourse. Both groups were composed of Eurosceptic parties, although while the nationalists were represented by right-wing Eurosceptic parties, the anti-austerians were represented by left-wing Eurosceptic parties. Nationalists rejected the relevant anti-crisis measures, pointing predominantly to national economic or political interests. They also tended to justify their positions in terms of Treaty articles that forbid bailouts. In their narrative, responsibility for the crisis is attributed to southern European states. In contrast, anti-austerians rejected the measures in question among other reasons because of solidarity with citizens of southern European states. These parties argued that decision-makers were burdening ordinary people with the costs of the crisis, whereas individual and institutional actors responsible for causing the crisis have not been held responsible. The chapter also provides numerous examples of parliamentary parties' discourses.

Chapter 6 investigates the macroeconomic preferences of national parliamentary parties. In the first step, the chapter maps which parties opted for neoliberal and which for Keynesian policies. In the second step, the chapter tests whether political parties' macroeconomic preferences can still be explained in terms of their position on the economic left–right dimension.

Neoliberal and Keynesian approaches differ significantly with regard to the role the state should play in the market cycle. In general, neoliberals stress deregulation, whereas Keynesians advocate the active role of the state in monetary and fiscal policy. Although both neoliberals and Keynesians share the assumption that markets act rationally, neoliberals argue that markets always get the price right, provided all the relevant information is publically available. Keynesians, by contrast, point to various 'market failures' which distort perfect competition.

Keynesians and neoliberals recommend different anti-crisis remedies: neoliberal economists advocate pro-cyclical measures and Keynesians counter-cyclical ones. According to Keynesians, governments should stimulate the economy by conducting expansionary fiscal and monetary policy, among other things, by increasing government spending, allowing inflation to rise and cutting taxes. In contrast, neoliberal economists argue that government spending is counterproductive during recessions because it tends to lead to stagflation (inflation and unemployment increase, while growth decreases). Instead, neoliberals suggest budgetary consolidation, austerity policies that aim at reducing public spending.

The chapter poses the following research question: do economic principles inform political parties' choices regarding anti-crisis measures in the eurozone or, on the contrary, is it the newly emerged conflict of interest between creditor and debtor states? The literature suggests that parties representing the economic 'left' are more likely to advocate Keynesian measures, whereas parties representing the economic 'right' favour neoliberal ones. However, the current political discourse in the eurozone suggests that the choice of anti-crisis policies rather reflects the conflict of interests between euro states that have received a bailout (debtors) and those that only provided financial guarantees (creditors). The empirical findings, based on (1) discourse analysis of national parliamentary debates and (2) the QCA model (crisp set), demonstrate that – besides a party's economic stance – receipt of a bailout also accounts for parliamentary parties' positioning on anti-crisis measures. In particular, parliamentary parties in debtor states are likely to opt for Keynesian anti-crisis measures, despite their right-wing economic stance or government membership.

The findings presented in this chapter demonstrate that the financial interdependence of states in the shared currency realm has generated a new mechanism that guides political parties' positioning on macroeconomic policies. As the empirical data demonstrate, parties from states that have received a bailout are particularly likely to propose macroeconomic measures that reflect their interests as debtor states: in other words, despite their right-wing economic orientation or government membership, parliamentary parties from bailout states opted for Keynesian measures. The second mechanism of political parties' positioning confirmed the existing knowledge based on the analysis of single currency systems. According to the literature, macroeconomic policy outcomes depend on a party's economic stance. That mechanism was clearly dominant among creditor states in which parliamentary parties were not affected by a crisis-specific logic of positioning.

Finally, Chapter 7 presents concluding remarks and suggests directions for further research. The chapter begins by interpreting the empirical findings of the other chapters. In the final section, the chapter returns to the question posed in the introductory chapter and attempts to evaluate national parliaments' role in the reform of European economic governance.

Notes

1 Starting from an infringement of the subsidiarity principle.
2 Bicameral parliaments obtain two votes (one vote for each chamber). In the area of freedom, security and justice a quarter of the total number of votes is sufficient to trigger a yellow card.
3 Author's italics.
4 Not all national parliaments are consulted ex ante by their governments. However, even if parliaments are not formally consulted, parliamentary parties can still find ways to communicate their preferences to the government.
5 BVerfG 09/07/2011, BVerfG 02/28/2012, BVerfG 06/3ß/2012, BVerfG 09/12/2012.

2 European financial crisis
Dominant narratives and the legal status of anti-crisis measures

The European financial crisis

When does the narrative of the European financial crisis start? Is it with the first bailout loan granted to Greece in May 2010, the introduction of the European Stimulus Plan in November 2008 or the bankruptcy of Lehman Brothers, announced on 15 September 2008? A subsequent question concerns the *nature* of the European financial crisis. In particular, has it been a financial crisis, a banking crisis, a sovereign debt crisis, a crisis of trade imbalances or a mortgage crisis? Moreover, can we consider the European crisis an extension of the global financial crisis or as an entirely different phenomenon? None of these views are wrong. The European crisis is a multi-faceted phenomenon produced by a combination of factors: the financial meltdown of 2007, the weaknesses of the banking system, governments' budgetary politics, but also, or even foremost, the institutional weakness of the Economic and Monetary Union (EMU) (Dyson, 2000).

The common currency was introduced in the European Union even though many economists and political scientists argued that the EU is not yet an optimum currency area (Enderlein and Verdun, 2009; Krugman, 2012). In particular, it has been observed that the eurozone meets only two out of three necessary conditions for establishing a common currency zone. While it is true that (1) labour mobility is guaranteed in the Treaties[1] (Article 45 of the Treaty) and (2) the member states of the eurozone conduct most of their trade with each other, there is no fiscal integration. In particular, the eurozone is a monetary, but not a transfer, union, meaning that redistribution and taxation remain within the competence of particular member states.

However, European decision-makers were convinced that the peer pressure alone would be sufficient to maintain fiscal disciple along the lines laid down in the Stability and Growth Pact (Enderlein and Verdun, 2009) (Dyson, 2000), (Heipertz and Verdun 2005). Hence, a fully-fledged fiscal union was not considered necessary. First of all, a common currency was economically attractive: given the fact that the member states conduct most of their trade with each other, the introduction of the euro was supposed to make cross-border business less expensive and less complicated. Uncertainties related to fluctuating exchange rates were simply eliminated. However, there are also disadvantages due to membership in the common currency; in particular, governments can no longer devalue their currency in order to foster domestic competitiveness. The only option available is so-called 'internal devaluation', which entails direct cuts in wages.

Finally, the eurozone was not conceived as an exclusively economic but also as a political project (Dyson and Featherstone, 1999; McNamara, 1999). The expectation was that the euro would strengthen the perception of the European Union as an entity and deepen European citizens' attachment to it (Risse, 2014). The political incentives have, therefore, played an important role in the process.

The global financial crisis erupted in the United States and later spilled over to Europe, affecting first of all its banking system. Accounting for the causes of the global financial crisis in 2007, Campbell (2010: 85) observed,

> Many of these reforms were rooted in the rising prominence of neoliberalism as the guiding light for US regulatory policy. The rise of neoliberalism was driven in large part by the financial services industry, especially on Wall Street, and their powerful allies in Washington.

Probably the most direct cause of the financial crisis was the trend towards deregulation in the housing market and risky lending practices. The policy of cheap credit increased the availability of sub-prime mortgages – that is, mortgages granted to people with a poor debt-to-income ratio. After the bursting of the housing bubble in the United States, defaults on sub-prime mortgages became very frequent. For instance, by September 2008 the average price of houses in the United States had decreased by 20 percent, meaning that borrowers who defaulted on their loans could not repay the whole sum owed by selling the property.

The development of the shadow banking system has been recognized as another major cause of the global financial crisis (Campbell, 2010). Shadow banking entities are financial companies that operate in market segments previously dominated by 'standard' banks. However, shadow banking entities are not subject to the same regulatory practices concerning, for instance, the level of deposits, as standard banks. Due to that difference, shadow banking proliferated and boosted the proportion of risky operations. For instance, the Lehman Brothers investment bank, which declared bankruptcy on 15 September 2008, has been criticized for pursuing particularly risky operations in the sub-prime market. The federal government decided not to bail out the bank in order to manifest its condemnation of its prior risky practices.

In the United States and Europe decision-makers responded to the crisis with a fiscal stimulus. In Europe, in November 2008 the European Commission proposed the European Economic Recovery Plan,[2] aimed at alleviating the effects of the global financial crisis. The plan, envisaged for two years, was financed from national budgets, the EU budget and the European Investment Bank. The recommendation was to implement a fiscal stimulus amounting to 1.5 percent of GDP. Furthermore, the Commission allowed EU member states to violate the criteria of the Stability and Growth Pack, for instance, by running higher deficits. The European Central Bank lowered its interest rates in order to stimulate the demand for credit. Most member states lowered taxes and introduced measures supporting green technologies or green initiatives such as scrappage programmes, which offered rebates for taxpayers willing to scrap their old, non-environmentally friendly vehicles in order to purchase modern ones. In practice, the amounts of fiscal stimulus introduced in the EU member states varied substantially. Few states opted for more substantial packages exceeding 2 percent of GDP; for instance, the sum of two packages introduced in Germany represented around 3 percent of GDP, in the United Kingdom the fiscal stimulus amounted to 2.2 percent of GDP, while in Spain it reached around 8 percent of GDP.

The European financial crisis manifested itself in 2009 with a rapid increase in interest rates on certain governments' bonds. This increase was caused by investors' concerns about debt sustainability in particular member states of the eurozone. Although by the end of 2009 the financial crisis still remained limited to Greece, a few months later it extended to other countries, namely, Ireland, Portugal, Spain and eventually Cyprus.

Over time it has become apparent that, in terms of the causes of the financial crisis, Greece constitutes a special, not a representative, case (Featherstone, 2011). Whereas in Greece the economic deterioration can be partly attributed to successive governments' fiscal mismanagement[3] or the large underground economy (Dell'Anno et al., 2007; Buehn and Schneider, 2011), Spain had a comparatively low level of debt at the beginning of the crisis (2010), at only 53 percent of GDP. However, in the first two years of the crisis the focus was often put on governments' irresponsibility, which ignores structural factors responsible for the European crisis. The dominant discourse of that time is well illustrated in the speech of a Belgian MP, who observed that *'It is difficult to maintain solidarity with those who have not adhered to the rules of financial transparency and made the figures look much better than they are.'*[4]

In the initial period of the crisis, decision-makers recognized skyrocketing interest rates on government bonds as the most disturbing symptom.

The main efforts, therefore, concentrated on winning back market confidence and helping states in crisis to maintain liquidity. While the key trigger of the crisis was declared to be overspending, the major remedy was austerity policies. By the same token, the member states of the eurozone initiated a change in the dominant paradigm from Keynesian policy-making to neoliberalism.

It has been observed that the Greek government-debt crisis was triggered indirectly by the global financial crisis of 2007, the structural weaknesses of the Greek economy, as evident in its low competitiveness and demand-led growth model, risky practices by French and German banks as well as the fiscal irresponsibility of Greek governments. The leading sectors of the Greek economy, namely, tourism and shipping, were severely affected by the global crisis. Imports and exports have decreased worldwide, which affected Greek companies involved in commerce (predominantly companies transporting goods with container vessels). Furthermore, the global economic downturn had a negative effect on tourism revenues, which fell by 15 percent in 2009. Although Greece recorded growth after the introduction of the euro (around 4 percent each year), the country continued to run high deficits, above 3 percent of GDP. It has been observed that the following factors were likely to contribute to deficits; persistently high public expenditure, imports of military equipment amounting to 8 percent of GDP,[5] as well as inability of the state bureaucracy to collect tax revenues (Buehn et al., 2011).

In February 2010 the newly elected government of George Papandreou realized that the Greek debt was higher than previously reported. The government admitted that flawed statistical practices were in place before it was elected. As a result, it was reported that the deficit did not amount to around 6 percent of GDP, as previously estimated, but rather 12 percent. Only two months later, the deficit calculated according to Eurostat's standardized method was already reported as 15.7 percent of GDP. The credit rating agencies severely downgraded Greek bonds, which made it impossible for Greece to finance itself on the open market. On 23 April 2010, Prime Minister Papandreou, in a speech from the island of Kastelorizo, acknowledged the need for external help:

> I have asked our partners to contribute decisively in order to give Greece a safe harbor. At the same time, we are sending a strong message to the markets that the EU is serious about protecting its common interest and common currency.[6]

The call for European solidarity was not widely acknowledged as legitimate; there were even voices suggesting that Greece sell its islands, but these suggestions were immediately rejected by the Prime Minister, who said that *'There are more imaginative and effective ways of dealing with the deficit than selling off Greek islands.'*[7] Eventually, in May 2010 representatives of the European Commission, European Central Bank and the International Monetary Fund launched a bailout loan of 110 billion euros in order to prevent a Greek default. The loan was made conditional on fulfilment of the Memorandum of Understanding (MoE) specifying the reforms that had to be undertaken in Greece. With the worsening economic situation at the end of 2011 it became necessary to support Greece with another bailout loan of 130 billion euros. Bondholders also accepted an extended maturity on bonds as well as lower interest rates.

In January 2015 left-wing party Syriza won the national elections in Greece. Greek voters placed their trust in the party that promised to bring an end to austerity. However, the national governments of euro states and the Commission were not willing to accept a reduction of the Greek debt. The political conflict escalated in summer 2015, with Prime Minister Alexis Tsipras announcing a referendum in which the Greek people were asked to decide whether their state should accept the bailout conditions laid down on 25 June by the Commission. On 5 July 2015, the Greek people rejected the conditions, with 61 percent voting against. The no-vote has not helped the Greek government to renegotiate better financial conditions. On the contrary, the bailout package accepted on 13 July by the Greek government contained more severe cuts in pensions and tax increases than the initial package rejected in the referendum.

In Ireland the 1990s were the period of the 'Celtic Tiger', when the country experienced an extraordinary economic growth fuelled predominantly by investment in high technology and the pharmaceutical sector. Although in the late 1990s and early 2000s the Irish economy experienced a slowdown, growth was maintained due to policies oriented towards attracting foreign companies, predominantly from the financial sector. In particular, during that period the government attracted foreign companies by very low corporation tax, deregulation and weak surveillance of the banking sector, low interest rates and a credit-friendly environment. These policies fuelled growth through high tax revenues: investment, particularly in the real estate sector, generated many new jobs. As a consequence, unemployment decreased and the Irish labour market accommodated many new workers, who also contributed to growth with their taxes. In the years preceding the global financial crisis Ireland had the lowest ratio of national debt to GDP in the whole eurozone.

However, the global financial crisis profoundly affected the Irish banking system. It has been estimated that in the years preceding the banking crisis the liabilities of Irish banks represented over 300 percent of GDP (Mair,

2011). Banks were extravagant in their lending to property developers and individual consumers; as a result, in the late 2000s the level of private debt in Ireland became very high. With the global financial crisis, the property bubble burst. The major Irish banks – the Anglo Irish Bank, the Bank of Ireland and Allied Irish Bank – which were involved in extensive lending, started losing deposits and were threatened by a loss of liquidity. When the Anglo Irish Bank announced a cash shortfall of 12 billion euros in September 2008, it found itself on the verge of bankruptcy. Faced with growing speculation, the Irish government announced a guarantee of all liabilities of the troubled banks. At that time, the total size of banks' liabilities has been estimated at around 334 billion euros, while Irish GDP was estimated at around 160 billion euros. When the private debt was transformed into public debt, the credit rating of Irish bonds fell and the government had to ask for a bailout loan. The loan was for 85 billion euros and consisted of loans from the bailout fund, the National Pension Reserve Fund and bilateral loans. In return, the Irish government agreed to introduce measures designed to reduce the national debt.

In Spain the major factor contributing to the crisis was the housing bubble. In the years preceding the crisis Spain had low debt, at only 53 percent of GDP. However, the demand-led growth model, combined with easy access to credit for individual consumers, contributed to a deterioration of the economic situation in 2009. As in the United States, the housing bubble was generated by a combination of rapidly growing house prices, banks' extravagance in granting credits to individual clients and government incentives, such as tax deductions on mortgages. It is estimated that real estate prices in Spain increased by 200 percent between 1996 and 2007. Spanish banks also invested in sub-prime mortgages and the level of Spanish household mortgage debt became one of the highest in the European Union. As a result of the global financial crisis of 2007 Spain fell into prolonged recession, which brought about a rapid increase in unemployment. This unemployment triggered a wave of defaults on sub-prime mortgages, which destabilized the banking system in Spain. In May 2012 the largest mortgage bank, Bankia, experienced severe losses from unpaid mortgages and, in order to avoid bankruptcy, it was nationalized. However, as other banks were also seriously affected by individual clients' defaults, the Spanish government obtained a 100 billion euro recapitalization package for Spanish banks from the European Financial Stability Facility (EFSF) in June 2012.

The demand-led growth model which dominated the decade before the crisis was fuelled by low interest rates on government bonds and the inflow of capital from northern European countries. The capital was employed predominantly to finance investments in real estate. Therefore, although in the pre-crisis decade Spain already had high expenditure, the economy was growing thanks to high tax revenues, to which the booming construction sector contributed significantly. However, already in 2004 Spain experienced a significant trade deficit, meaning that the monetary value of imports was higher than the monetary value of exports.

Two factors contributed to generating a trade deficit in Spain: wage increases and demand-driven growth (Hall, 2014). After the introduction of the euro, Spain experienced a fall in unemployment and a rapid increase in wages. As a result, domestic consumption also increased significantly and helped to generate growth through increased tax revenues. However, high wages decreased the competitiveness of Spanish production, which became more expensive. This trend had far-reaching consequences. Namely, growing labour costs usually motivate investors to relocate production to cheaper regions. Furthermore, wage increases are also reflected in the cost of exported products, which become more expensive. If there are other producers on the market that offer the same product for a lower price, the producer in question is likely to lose that market.

At the same time, in the decade preceding the crisis, Germany oriented its economy towards an export-led model in which growth is generated through trade surpluses (Hall, 2014). The implementation of the strategy became possible due to two important conditions. First, Germany exports technologically advanced and innovative products. Second, in order to foster the competitiveness of its exported goods, German wages were suppressed in order to keep prices low. By comparison, after the introduction of the euro, Spanish wages increased more rapidly than German ones. The global financial crisis has also affected the German economy, but not to a similar extent as in southern Europe. In particular, German exports to southern Europe decreased, but the gap could be compensated through trade with Asia. Southern Europe, relying on a demand-led growth model, had no alternative options at its disposal but to pursue internal devaluation in order to regain competitiveness. Devaluation is the most common strategy for bringing a trade deficit under control. If the national currency loses value in relation to other currencies, the debt generated through trade deficit decreases and the competitiveness of the country can be boosted because its exports become cheaper. In the eurozone, devaluation is not available; governments of states running trade deficits have to pursue internal devaluation in order to re-establish the trade balance. Along these lines, the Spanish government decreased wages, liberalized the labour market and increased taxes.

In Portugal the financial crisis was triggered predominantly by bad banking practices. The two major banks – Banco Português de Negócios (BPN) and Banco Privado Português (BPP) – accumulated losses due to risky investments and fraud, which came to light in the turmoil of the financial crisis. The global financial crisis of 2007 also weakened the banking system. In 2008, Portugal, like other EU member states, introduced a fiscal stimulus. The expenditure was reflected in the deficit of 2009, which reached 9.4 percent of GDP. Like other states whose deficits increased either due to fiscal stimulus or purchases of banks' share capital, investors downgraded the government's bonds. When the 10-year government bond reached 7 percent, the Portuguese government decided to ask for a bailout loan. In September 2010 the austerity package for Portugal was announced, mainly comprising measures of internal devaluation, such as reduction of labour costs. Furthermore, the austerity plan also introduced measures oriented towards reducing the deficit, such as tax increases.

The Cypriot economy has been particularly affected by external developments, such as the global financial crisis of 2007 and the Greek financial crisis of 2010. Due to the global financial crisis Cyprus experienced losses in tourism and shipping, which contributed to the growth of unemployment. Furthermore, in that period the average value of properties decreased by 30 percent. In 2010 Cyprus' major banks – Cyprus Popular Bank (also known as LAIKI), the Bank of Cyprus and the Hellenic Bank – found themselves on the verge of collapse due to exposure to the Greek financial crisis. In the decade preceding the European financial crisis, Cypriot banks invested considerably in Greek bonds and thus experienced losses when depositors had to accept lower interest and extended maturity on Greek bonds.

However, the major trigger of the financial crisis in Cyprus was the oversized banking industry and particularly the offshore banking sector. In the 2000s banks attracted many depositors by offering them very good conditions. As a consequence, Cyprus, a state with a small population and a small economy, grew a very large banking industry. As a consequence, in Cyprus bank assets are estimated at a multiple of eight times GDP, amounting to 19 billion euros in 2011 (Begg, 2013). Out of 41 banks operating in Cyprus on the verge of the crisis in 2012, only 6 were local. Offshore banks, constituting a substantial share of banks in Cyprus, were estimated to hold assets worth approximately 82 billion US dollars. Offshore banks are banks located outside the country of residence of the depositors, usually in low-tax areas or so-called tax havens. For instance, in Cyprus a large share of the foreign deposits belong to wealthy Russians. Offshore banks are attracted by exemption from the local regulatory environment and taxes. In return, they offer more secrecy to their clients and higher interest rates. However, because the states in which offshore banks are located usually do not insure the deposits, their holders risk losing their savings if a given offshore bank defaults.

After the Cyprus Popular Bank (LAIKI) – the largest bank in Cyprus – experienced severe losses, due predominantly to the 'haircut' on Greek deposits, it was downgraded by credit rating agencies and, as a result, lost liquidity. In order to prevent a default, the government covered the capital deficit of 1.8 billion euros and acquired 84 percent of its share capital. The bank was thus nationalized. The increase in debt caused by recapitalization of the Cyprus Popular Bank led to a downgrading of the government's bonds in June 2012 to BB+ (for long-term assessments) and B (for short-term assessments). The Republic of Cyprus then asked for a bailout loan. The 10 billion euro loan was conditional on the implementation of a general haircut (cut in interest rates) on deposits. However, the national parliament rejected the measure in March 2013. Eventually, the haircut was approved only for uninsured deposits of more than 100,000 euros.

The legal status of anti-crisis measures

Anti-crisis measures had very different kinds of legal status, encompassing acts under international private law, intergovernmental agreements, a treaty amendment (Article 136.3 TFEU), regulations and directives, but also country-specific recommendations of a dubious legal nature. As a consequence, the procedures for their approval also differed. Furthermore, governments also influenced the approval procedures by merging two measures and submitting them in that form for parliamentary discussion and vote. The implication was that parliaments could have one vote in order to decide on two different measures simultaneously. In this section we briefly present the legal status, content and mode of approval of the measures analyzed.

The EFSF was established with the EFSF framework agreement as a private company based in Luxembourg, outside the EU legal framework. Member states did not foresee its incorporation into the Treaty, although they envisaged taking this step later with its successor, the European Stability Mechanism (ESM) (De Witte, 2011). The legality of the EFSF has been disputed. In particular, critics questioned the legal basis for the EFSF (private company established outside EU law). Furthermore, referring to both the European Financial Stabilization Mechanism (EFSM)[8] and the EFSF, critics noted that Article 122(2) refers to cases of 'natural disasters or exceptional occurrences beyond its control' (Ruffert, 2011), whereas maintaining budgetary discipline cannot be recognized as being *beyond* governments' control.

However, there were also legal experts who maintained that the EFSF does not breach the no-bailout clause (Haede, 2009; Louis, 2010; Seyad, 2010). First, the financial assistance offered to member states would only be temporary due to the extraordinary character of the situation, and second, Article 122 does not explicitly prohibit financial assistance, and the provision is relatively open regarding the means by which it could be provided.

The establishment of the European Financial Stability Facility (EFSF), as well as the increase of its budgetary capacity, required the unanimous approval of all eurozone member states. Although the EFSF constituted an intergovernmental agreement under private law (the EFSF was established as a private company owned by the governments of the eurozone states), the measure was approved by a ratification procedure, otherwise reserved for international agreements.

In contrast to the temporary EFSF, the European Stability Mechanism (ESM) has a less precarious legal basis (De Witte, 2011). In particular, it was established as an intergovernmental organization with the Treaty Establishing the European Stability Mechanism. The ESM became the permanent bailout fund and continues to fulfil the same goals as the temporary EFSF. The European Council of 25 March 2011, acting in unanimity, and following the procedure of Article 48(6), adapted Decision 2011/119/EU amending Article 136(3) TFEU by inserting the following text:

> The member states whose currency is the euro may establish a stability mechanism to be activated if indispensable to safeguard the stability of the euro as a whole. The granting of any required financial assistance under the mechanism will be made subject to strict conditionality.

The new measure was introduced through the simplified treaty revision procedure; hence, with minor involvement of the European Parliament or national parliaments in the drafting process. The Lisbon Treaty introduced a simplified procedure for amending policies and internal actions of the EU. Under that procedure the convening of a European Convention and an Intergovernmental Conference can be avoided. However, with that procedure EU competences may not be extended. In contrast to the EFSF, the ESM was able to enter into force after being ratified by states representing 90 percent of its capital requirements, as stipulated in the funding Treaty Establishing the European Stability Mechanism.

The Treaty on Stability, Coordination and Governance in the Economic and Monetary Union (TSCG), as an international agreement outside EU law, was signed on 2 March 2012, by all governments of the EU member states except the United Kingdom, the Czech Republic and Croatia. The Fiscal Compact is a stricter version of the previous Stability and Growth Pact. Member states bound by the treaty are required to introduce into domestic law (preferably at the constitutional level) a self-correcting mechanism which shall guarantee that their national budgets are balanced. In particular, the general budget deficit shall not exceed 3 percent of GDP, the structural deficit shall be less than 1 percent of GDP and the debt-to-GDP ratio shall remain below 60 percent.

According to Article 14(2) and (3), the TSCG had to be ratified by at least 12 Eurozone member states in order to enter into force. The objective was reached by January 1, 2013, after Austria, Cyprus, Germany, Estonia, Spain, France, Greece, Italy, Ireland, Portugal, Finland and Slovenia ratified the treaty. However, the ratification procedures varied significantly across states. In Ireland, for example, the treaty was subject to popular referendum (which took place on 31 May 2012) while in Cyprus it was ratified by an act of government, hence, without consulting the national parliament. In other states, national parliaments were requested to authorize the ratification of the Treaty.

The ratification process of the Fiscal Compact, as well as the amendment of Article 136(3), took place under conditionality pressure. According to the Memoranda of Understanding, loans can be made on condition that the debtor state ratifies the Fiscal Compact. Under those circumstances, several states – such as Greece, Italy or France – opted to combine ratification of the two treaties with amendment of Article 136(3). For national parliaments this decision implied that they had to approve or reject the three legal documents with one vote.

The entry into force of directives and regulations does not require a national parliamentary ratification procedure. However, in most eurozone states the two-pack and the six-pack were debated together with the ESM or the Fiscal Compact (as a package). These two packages are aimed at strengthening the procedures for reducing public deficits and addressing macroeconomic imbalances. All 28 EU member states are committed by the Stability and Growth Pact to implement a fiscal policy designed to keep within the limits on the government deficit (3 percent of GDP) and debt (60 percent of GDP). Four of the six instruments in the six-pack are used to further reform the Stability and Growth Pact, focussing on improving compliance.[9] These reforms do not change any of the conditions already imposed by the Pact but aim to enforce greater budgetary discipline among the member states of the euro area by stipulating that sanctions shall come into force earlier and more consistently. For example, when a country against which an excessive deficit procedure has been opened fails to take measures prescribed to eliminate its deficit, an interest-bearing deposit equalling 0.2 percent of GDP is payable. With continued non-compliance the deposit is converted into a fine. In addition, automatic sanctions are triggered based on a different voting mechanism in the Council of the European Union (Reverse Qualified Majority Voting). At the same time, the national accounts statistics and forecasting practices of member states are adjusted to comply with EU standards. If it is determined that a country has reported false data, an additional fine may be imposed. The remaining two pieces of legislation in the six-pack concern the Macroeconomic Imbalance Procedure, an early warning system and correction mechanism for excessive macroeconomic imbalances.[10] It is designed to prevent or correct risky macroeconomic developments, such as high current account deficits, unsustainable external indebtedness and housing bubbles.

The two-pack consists of two regulations[11] on monitoring budgetary plans. Regulation 473/2013 stipulates that states which are neither under an Excessive Deficit Procedure (EDP) nor an Excessive Imbalance Procedure (EIP) nor a Financial Assistance Programme are obliged to present their budget to the Commission by October 15 each year. The Commission's opinion is supposed to be debated in national parliaments before the final budget is approved. Although the Commission does not have any veto power over national parliaments, it can issue warnings if a draft budget violates the Fiscal Compact. Regulation 472/2013 stipulates the conditions for enhanced surveillance applying to states under financial assistance. In that case the reports are to be submitted on a quarterly basis and the Commission is entitled to send warnings to national parliaments if the state in question does not comply with the conditionality.

Conclusions

This chapter is composed of two sections: the first one highlights the variety of factors that led to the financial meltdown in the European Union and the United States; the second section presents the legality of tools that have been introduced in the European Union in order to counter the effects of the crisis. The first section provides, therefore, more than a narrative of events; rather, it concentrates on demonstrating the complexity and diversity of factors that eventually led to the financial crisis. The second section, in turn, presents the 'institutional' response to the crisis.

In the initial phase of the financial crisis various political actors or the media tended to simplify the causes of the crisis attributing it generally to irresponsible fiscal politics of governments. The process has been labelled as 'hellenization' of the crisis. However, with time it became clear that the causes of the crisis were more complex. In the United States the crisis could be attributed to deregulation in the housing market as well as risky lending practices in the banking sectors. The European financial crisis manifested itself in 2009 with a rapid increase in interest rates on mainly southern European governments' bonds. Investors were increasingly concerned about debt sustainability in these states. However, Greece constitutes an exceptional rather than a representative case. In Greece the financial crisis could be, next to risky banking practices by French and German banks, attributed to fiscal mismanagement and large underground economy. In Ireland the crisis has been predominantly caused by risky lending practices of banks and a huge property bubble. In Spain the causes of the financial crisis were all different from Greece. In particular, before the crisis public finances in Spain were healthy. The size of the underground economy has been neither exceptionally large. However, easy access to consumer credits led to a housing bubble. In Portugal the crisis has been generated predominantly by risky investment and bad practices in the banking sector. Finally, in Cyprus the financial destabilization can be attributed to over-sized banking industry and, in particular, a large offshore banking sector.

In order to counter the effects of the crisis but also in order to prevent a new one, various new institutional tools were implemented. This book concentrates the major ones, namely, the temporary (the European Financial Stability Facility) and the permanent bailout funds (the European Stability Mechanism) as well as the reformed version of the Stability and Growth Pact. The general goal of the bailout funds has been to provide financial liquidity to EU member states whose currency is euro. The EFSF is claimed to have a precarious legal basis, namely, was established as a private company based in Luxembourg, outside the EU legal framework. The ESM became the permanent bailout fund and continues to fulfil the same goals as the temporary EFSF. The Treaty on Stability, Coordination and Governance in the Economic and Monetary Union (also referred to as the Fiscal Compact), as an international agreement outside EU law, was signed on March 2, 2012, by all governments of the EU member states except the United Kingdom, the Czech Republic and Croatia. The Fiscal Compact introduced a stricter and a more coordinated control of national budgets but also economic policies. The Fiscal Compact provided the European Commission as well as the Council with new surveillance powers in that policy area.

Notes

1 Some commentators have also noted that high linguistic diversity in the European Union de facto prevents labour mobility.
2 http://ec.europa.eu/economy_finance/publications/publication13504_en.pdf
3 According to Eurostat, in 2009 Greek public debt reached 127 percent of GDP.
4 H. Bogaert MP, Belgium, national parliament, 13.09.2011.
5 Greece has traditionally devoted around 8 percent of the budget to military equipment imported predominantly from the United States, Germany and France. According to NATO statistics, Greece has been the second-biggest defence spender globally after the United States.
6 www.content.time.com
7 *New York Times*, 05.10.2012 Greece won't sell islands to cover debts, R. Mackey.

8 The EFSM, established by Directive 407/2010, uses the budget of the EU as collateral (60 billion euros). In contrast, the EFSF (440 billion euros) is a fund in which capital guarantees are granted by euro states.
9 Regulation 1175/2011 amending Regulation 1466/97, Regulation 1177/2011 amending Regulation 1467/97, Regulation 1173/2011, Directive 2011/85/EU.
10 Regulation 1176/2011, Regulation 1174/2011.
11 Regulation 473/2013, Regulation 472/2013.

3 Empowered or disempowered?

The role of national parliaments during the reform of European economic governance

Introduction

This chapter investigates how the intergovernmental reform process of European economic governance affected national parliaments' oversight of that policy area. The chapter addresses the following questions: which parliaments became disempowered and which managed to secure their formal powers? What domestic and international factors contributed to the (dis)empowerment of national parliaments? What consequences do the observed practices have on the quality of democratic control in European economic governance?

The chapter examines how national parliaments in all eurozone states were involved in approving the following measures: the European Financial Stability Facility (EFSF), both its establishment and the increase of its budgetary capacity; the European Stability Mechanism (ESM); and the Treaty on Stability, Coordination and Governance in the Economic and Monetary Union. The dependent variable of the study is operationalized as the presence or absence of so-called 'emergency legislation' or 'fast-track procedures' that allow governments to accelerate the legislative process and minimize the risk of a default by constraining national parliaments' powers. Fast-track procedures are applied in exceptional situations requiring rapid legal output. They shorten the legislative process and limit the involvement of national parliaments (for instance, it is a common practice in many states to accelerate the approval process by limiting the number of parliamentary readings from three to one). Another manifestation of emergency legislation is a legislative merger. Mergers constitute legal packages comprising two or more bills submitted to a national parliament for discussion and vote. Parliaments have only one vote at their disposal in order to approve or reject the whole legal package.

In the empirical dimension, this chapter systematically maps patterns of national parliaments' (dis)empowerment during the reform process of economic governance and demonstrates what domestic and international factors explain the variation. The findings demonstrate that whereas northern European parliaments' powers were secured (or in some cases even fostered), southern European parliaments became disempowered due to the following factors: (1) domestic constitutional set-up allowing implementation of fast-track measures, (2) national supreme or constitutional courts' consent to extensive application of emergency legislation and (3) international economic and political pressure on governments in southern European states to prevent default in the approval process. Due to significant power asymmetries national parliaments remained *de jure* but not *de facto* equal in the exercise of their control powers at the EU level. As a consequence, both the disempowerment of particular parliaments and the asymmetry of powers in the collective dimension had a negative effect on the legitimacy of European economic governance.

This chapter begins by presenting shortly the empirical database developed for this study and the anti-crisis measures analyzed. In the next section the chapter presents the analytical framework, which concentrates on the role of national parliamentary oversight of European policy-making. Having defined emergency legislation, the chapter proceeds by presenting the empirical evidence on the dominant patterns of national parliaments' (dis) empowerment and the impact of domestic and international factors. In the concluding section the chapter discusses the empirical findings from a normative perspective.

The database

The empirical enquiry in this chapter is based on a database covering various patterns of approval/ratification procedures of major anti-crisis measures introduced in the eurozone between 2009 and 2013 (see Table 3.1 for a summary). The database provides information on how specific anti-crisis measures were approved in all eurozone member states. The measures under examination here are: the European Financial Stability Facility (EFSF), both its establishment and the increase of its budgetary capacity; the European Stability Mechanism (ESM); and the Treaty on Stability, Coordination and Governance in the Economic and Monetary Union. The database mapped the presence or absence of the following procedures accompanying the approval process of each anti-crisis measure: vote, plenary debate, merger and fast-track procedure. The database also provides further information on the number of plenary debates, as well as legislative acts that were merged either for the debate or a vote. The information was obtained directly from national parliaments.[1]

Table 3.1 Approvals of anti-crisis measures

Country	Anti-crisis measure	Vote	Debate	Merger	Fast-track procedure
Belgium	EFSF-1	yes	yes	no	no
	EFSF-2	yes	yes	no	no
	ESM	yes	yes	no	no
	FISCAL COMPACT	yes	yes	no	no
Spain	EFSF-1	yes	no	no	yes
	EFSF-2	yes	no	no	yes
	ESM	yes	yes	yes, with the decision to modify Article 136 TFEU (balanced budget rule)	no
	FISCAL COMPACT	yes	yes (only one)	no	yes
France	EFSF-1	yes	yes (only one)	yes, with the budget bill	yes
	EFSF-2	yes	yes (only one)		yes
	ESM	yes	yes (only one)	yes (with Article 136 TFEU)	yes
	FISCAL COMPACT	yes	yes (only one)	no	yes
Austria	EFSF-1	yes	yes	no	no
	EFSF-2	yes	yes	no	no
	ESM	yes	yes	no	no
	FISCAL COMPACT	yes	yes	no	no
Cyprus	EFSF-1	yes	yes	no	yes
	EFSF-2	yes	yes (only one)	no	yes
	ESM	yes	yes	no	no
	FISCAL COMPACT	no, approved with a gov. decree	no	no	no
Estonia	EFSF-1	Estonia was not in the eurozone at that time, therefore, not part of the EFSF in the beginning			

	EFSF-2	yes	no	no
	ESM	yes	no	no
	FISCAL COMPACT	yes	no	no
Finland	EFSF-1	yes	no	no
	EFSF-2	yes	no	no
	ESM	yes	no	no
	FISCAL COMPACT	yes	yes	no
Germany	EFSF-1	yes	no	no
	EFSF-2	yes	no	no
	ESM	yes	no	no
	FISCAL COMPACT	yes	no	no
Greece	EFSF-1	no	no	yes
	EFSF-2	yes	yes (law on property tax and regulation of bank supervision)	no
	ESM	yes	yes (with the Article 136(3) and the Fiscal Compact)	no
	FISCAL COMPACT	yes	yes (with the Article 136(3) and the Fiscal Compact)	no
Ireland	EFSF-1	yes	no	no
	EFSF-2	yes	no	no
	ESM	yes	no	no
	FISCAL COMPACT	debate, vote and referendum (60,29% in favour)	debate, vote and referendum (60,29% in favour)	no
Italy	EFSF-1	no (gov. decree)	no	yes
	EFSF-2	no (gov. decree)	no	yes

(*Continued*)

Table 3.1 (Continued)

Country	Anti-crisis measure	Vote	Debate	Merger	Fast-track procedure
	ESM	yes (Article 136(3)+ESM+Fiscal Compact)	yes	yes	no
	FISCAL COMPACT	yes (Article 136(3)+ESM+Fiscal Compact)	yes	yes	no
Luxembourg	EFSF-1	yes	yes	no	no
	EFSF-2	yes	yes	no	no
	ESM	yes	yes	no	no
	FISCAL COMPACT	yes	yes	no	no
Malta	EFSF-1	yes	yes	no	yes
	EFSF-2	yes	yes	no	yes
	ESM	yes (with the Article 136(3) TFEU)	yes	yes	no
	FISCAL COMPACT	debate and vote, (debate with the six-pack and the two-pack)	yes	no	no
Netherlands	EFSF-1	no	yes	no	yes
	EFSF-2	yes (with budgetary law)	yes	yes	yes
	ESM	yes (with Article 136(3) TFEU)	yes	yes	no
	FISCAL COMPACT	yes	yes	no	no
Portugal	EFSF-1	yes	yes	no	no
	EFSF-2	no (gov. decree)	no	no	yes
	ESM	yes	yes	(with the Article 136(3) TFEU)	no
	FISCAL COMPACT	yes	yes	no	no
Slovakia	EFSF-1	yes	yes	no	no
	EFSF-2	yes	yes	no	no
	ESM	yes	yes	no	no

Slovenia	FISCAL COMPACT	yes	yes	no
	EFSF-1	yes	yes	no
	EFSF-2	yes	yes	no
	ESM	yes	yes	no
	FISCAL COMPACT	yes	yes	no

Source: Based on the author's original research

The dependent variable of this study is defined as the application of emergency legislation in a given eurozone member state during the European financial crisis. This study aims to contribute to the literature with a systematic analysis of approvals of all major anti-crisis tools in all national parliaments of eurozone states. Although all the abovementioned measures belonged to the so-called 'reform package', their content and legal status differ substantially. The EFSF and ESM established a bailout fund to provide financial support to eurozone member states that could no longer finance themselves on the markets (due to liquidity or solvency problems). While the EFSF was established as a temporary solution, the ESM became a permanent bailout fund. The Fiscal Compact is a stricter version of the previous Stability and Growth Pact. Member states bound by the treaty are required to introduce into domestic law a self-correcting mechanism that is supposed to guarantee that their national budgets are balanced. In particular, the general budget deficit shall not exceed 3 percent of GDP, the structural deficit shall be less than 1 percent of GDP and the debt-to-GDP ratio shall remain below 60 percent. In general, while the EFSF and the ESM deepened financial solidarity in European economic governance, the Fiscal Compact strengthened budgetary surveillance.

The role of parliamentary oversight in European policy-making

The literature traditionally stresses the following core functions of national parliaments: law-making, representation of citizens and oversight (Blondel, 1973). However, at the European level, national parliaments are limited in the exercise of these three functions (Maurer and Wessels, 2001; O'Brennan and Raunio, 2007). While in domestic politics national parliaments enjoy the right to propose, amend, pass or reject bills, at the European level their impact is far more restricted (Mayoral, 2011). In particular, the Treaty has explicitly confirmed that the major functions of national parliaments in the European Union consist of, first, establishing a channel of accountability between the Council and national constituencies and, second, controlling the decision-making process at the EU level (Articles 10 and 12 of the TEU) (de Witte et al., 2010; Downson and de Witte, 2013). Against that background, in the reform process of European economic governance the competences of national parliaments consisted of controlling national governments' actions in that policy area and approving (but not drafting or amending) the legislation.

This study aims at establishing in which states national parliaments' formal oversight powers have been restricted and why. In this study oversight is broadly defined as 'the review, monitoring and supervision of government and public agencies, including the implementation of policy and legislation' (Born et al., 2007: 9–10). Adaptation of a broader definition of oversight allows us to capture better how the period of European financial crisis affected parliamentary oversight practices *beyond* scrutiny of governments' work. According to Born the key functions of parliamentary oversight are:

> to detect and prevent abuse (...) or unconstitutional conduct of government and public agencies, to hold government to account in respect of how taxpayers' money is used, to ensure that policies announced by the government and authorised by parliament are actually delivered and to improve the transparency of government operations.
>
> (Born et al., 2007: 9–10)

Forms of parliamentary oversight concern institutionalized activities through which national parliaments exercise their control, in particular: vote, plenary debate, written or oral questions and reports. We can differentiate between strictly and weakly formalized tools of oversight. The level of formalization can refer either to the very entitlement to use a given procedure or the frequency of its application. Voting and plenary debates are the two most powerful and most strictly formalized forms of parliamentary oversight. Both entitlement and the frequency with which these tools can be applied are strictly regulated by national secondary law. If national law requires a debate and a vote on a given measure, national parliaments are obliged to provide them. Plenary debates and voting are also procedurally formalized. For instance, the law specifies whether a given bill can be approved with a simple or a special majority. Furthermore, the law also stipulates the required number of plenary debates (usually distinguished as the first, second or third reading). If a national parliament is composed of two chambers, the order of plenary debates and voting is also strictly regulated.

During the European financial crisis national and supranational executive institutions experienced an increase of power in European economic governance: the Council and national governments became the locus of decision-making (Hefftler et al., 2013, 2015). At the same time, the increase of power on the executive side was not accompanied with a corresponding increase of control powers by the European and national parliaments (Lord, 2012). On the contrary, parliaments were hardly represented in that process: the European Parliament was basically excluded while national parliaments played only a consultative role (Fasone, 2014a).

The distancing of parliaments from the reform process has been attributed to a considerable time pressure requiring prompt entry into force of the new legislation. Governments wanted to ensure that the measures agreed by them were also approved successfully at the domestic level. As a consequence, some governments turned to special fast-track procedures or merged the debated EU draft legislative acts in order to accelerate the legislative process but also to minimize the risk of a default. To what extent were national parliaments disempowered in the course of that process? There is no agreement in the literature. Whereas some studies maintain that parliaments' powers suffered (Lord, 2012; Crum, 2013) others contradict – to some extent – the disempowerment thesis (Benz, 2013; Auel and Hoeing, 2014; Fasone, 2014b; Rittberger, 2014). For instance, Fasone (2014b) and Benz (2013) observed that rulings of national or supreme courts have actually fostered selected national parliaments' control functions. We can explain the lack of consensus by the following factors: first, most studies focus on a limited number of cases or analyze the impact of one institution (for example, courts) on parliamentary oversight practice. Second, other studies analyze how effective parliaments were in making use of their already formally limited competences.

In contrast to the existing studies, this analysis covers all member states of the eurozone. Furthermore, the analysis does not focus selectively on the impact of one institution but rather considers the impact of both domestic and international factors. For the sake of coherence, the study concentrates on parliaments' formal powers in the approval (ratification) of these legislative measures but not their execution or management.[2]

Drawing on the literature, the study identifies the following factors that influence implementation of emergency legislation: domestic constitutional set-up, activity of supreme or constitutional courts and international (political and economic) pressure on national governments. First, national constitutions usually stipulate, albeit in general terms, how and when emergency legislation can be employed. As a result, in some states national parliaments' powers can be more constrained than in others. Constitutional set-up delineates the breadth and depth of the application of emergency legislation. In the first dimension, the national constitutional framework usually stipulates in which policy areas emergency legislation should be avoided. The second dimension concerns the possible level of national parliaments' disempowerment in the legislative process. Exclusion of parliaments can involve a reduction in the number of plenary debates but also the possibility of eliminating plenary debates or votes.

Second, constitutional and supreme courts decide whether a given application of emergency legislation is constitutional. However, as courts are embedded in a socio-political environment, their rulings can display different levels of independence. In particular, courts may be inclined to issue rulings supporting governments' preferences. Under these circumstances their interpretation of constitutional principles may not be entirely impartial. One indicator of courts' partiality can be a lack of coherence in their rulings over a short period of time. Third, due to international political or economic pressure governments may be more likely to limit parliaments' powers. In particular, external pressure can mobilize governments to pursue measures to ensure successful ratification.

Emergency legislation: conceptualization

Emergency legislation is codified in all European states. The common feature of all special procedures is that they shorten the usual period required for approval/ratification of legislation and limit the role of national legislatures in the process. These procedures constitute a deviation from standard procedure as they allow governments to pass laws without or with only limited involvement of national parliaments. Furthermore, national legislation does not always explicitly label emergency legislation as a fast-track procedure. In many states decree-laws fulfil the function of a fast-track procedure (see, for instance, Article 86 of the Spanish Constitution and Article 77 of the Italian Constitution). However, as these practices are exempted from any form of harmonization, there is a lot of variation among European states (for more details on practices regarding fast-track procedures see Cartabia et al., 2011).

Fast-track procedures are not undemocratic in themselves; on the contrary, they are necessary in order to deal with unexpected, large-scale urgencies, such as the management of natural disasters or terrorist attacks. These situations usually require a rapid reaction which should not be slowed down by lengthy legislative procedures. Therefore, it is considered good practice not to apply fast-track procedures to deal with predictable or flagged issues. Some experts even claim that the law should not codify circumstances under which fast-track procedures apply because the nature of such events is indefinable.[3] Nonetheless, in order to prevent abuse of fast-track procedures, most states usually stipulate when these procedures can be applied. For instance, the UK House of Lords in a report entitled 'Fast-Track Legislation: Constitutional Implications and Safeguards' notes that in the United Kingdom fast-track procedures are frequently employed unnecessarily. These decisions were often attributed to governments' desire to demonstrate their commitment to the public: 'It was another example of the Government wanting to be seen to be doing something. That legislation was put through for the optics, not because it was a genuine security requirement.'[4]

The House of Lords identified five principles that should underpin the application of fast-track procedures: (1) maintenance of effective parliamentary scrutiny, (2) the need to produce 'good law', (3) the need to maintain consultations with stakeholders, (4) respect for proportionality and appropriateness and (5) maintenance of transparency in the legislative process.[5]

In general, it can be observed that emergency legislation can limit parliaments' powers in both a vertical and a horizontal dimension. Vertically, we can differentiate different *grades* of parliaments' disempowerment. For instance, this study considers the following criteria:

1 Was the usual number of plenary debates reduced?
2 Were plenary debates entirely limited?
3 Was voting eliminated as well?

First, application of a fast-track procedure can entirely eliminate national parliaments from the legislative process, meaning that parliaments neither vote on nor debate a given bill; second, a fast-track procedure can eliminate parliamentary debate entirely but retain voting; and third, emergency legislation can reduce the usual number of debates (for instance, from three to one reading) and retain voting. Emergency legislation can also limit parliaments' powers in a horizontal dimension. In particular, national law may stipulate in which policy areas emergency legislation can or cannot be applied.

Another type of practice limiting national parliaments' powers in a horizontal dimension is a legislative merger. Governments merge two – or more – bills and present them as a legal package for parliamentary discussion and vote. The practice of mergers varies across European states. In some states it is common to accompany budgetary debates with related issues; in other states mergers are not at all frequent. That practice not only accelerates the approval process but also increases the likelihood of the bill's approval. That is particularly the case if the major element of the merger is an important piece of legislation which is in any case widely supported by parliamentary parties. Under these circumstances MPs are more likely to vote in favour because they have only one vote in order to approve or reject the whole legal package. Finally, application of emergency legislation is highly case-specific. Even if governments are entitled to pursue a fast-track procedure in a particular case, they may not make use of that right.

Application of emergency legislation during the European financial crisis – empirical evidence

Comparative empirical analysis clearly demonstrates one dominant tendency. Southern European parliaments' powers were more constrained than those of their northern European counterparts. The states that approved anti-crisis measures *without* employing any fast-track procedure or merger were: Belgium, Austria, Estonia, Finland, Germany, Ireland, Luxembourg, Slovakia and Slovenia. With the exception of Ireland, all the states belong to the group of so-called creditors. The other group of states – which comprised Spain, France, Cyprus, Greece, Italy, Malta, Netherlands and Portugal – approved European anti-crisis measures either with fast-track procedures or mergers. In the second group the outliers are France and the Netherlands.

The establishment of the European Financial Stability Facility (EFSF), as well as the increase of its budgetary capacity, required the unanimous approval of all eurozone member states. Although the EFSF constituted an intergovernmental agreement under private law, the measure was usually approved with a ratification procedure, reserved otherwise only for international agreements. The states that approved the establishment of the EFSF with a standard parliamentary ratification procedure were: Belgium, Austria, Finland, Germany, Ireland, Luxemburg, Portugal, Slovakia and Slovenia (see Table 3.1). In Spain the EFSF was approved via a fast-track procedure (decree-law) which envisaged a parliamentary vote but no plenary debate. In France, the EFSF was approved with a special procedure that reduced the number of readings to one. It was also incorporated into the budget bill and submitted to a parliamentary vote as a single package. In Cyprus and Malta the EFSF was also introduced with a special procedure accelerating the approval process but without cancelling the voting procedure and parliamentary discussion. Estonia was not a member of the eurozone at that time and thus did not participate in the approval process. Greece approved the EFSF with a fast-track procedure (government decree) without consulting the parliament in any form (there was neither debate nor vote). In Italy the EFSF framework agreement was implemented through Decree-Law (Decreto-legge) n. 78/2010 stipulating 'Urgent measures on financial stability and economic competitiveness'. As a consequence, there was neither a debate nor a vote accompanying the Decree-Law.[6]

Parliamentary involvement in the process of approving an increase in the budgetary capacity of the EFSF followed the same pattern across the analyzed states. As a result, it was predominantly creditor states that approved the increased budgetary capacity of the EFSF with a standard procedure: Belgium, Austria, Cyprus, Estonia, Finland, Germany, Ireland, Luxemburg, Slovakia and Slovenia. The role of the relevant parliaments was limited in Spain, France and Malta. In these states, parliaments voted on increasing the budgetary capacity of the EFSF, but the usual number of plenary debates was reduced. In Greece and in the Netherlands national parliaments debated and voted on a merger: in Greece approval of the EFSF was combined with the law on a property tax and regulation of bank supervision, whereas in the Netherlands it was merged with the budgetary law. In Portugal the parliament was not consulted in any form (government decree).

The Treaty Establishing the European Stability Mechanism has been ratified according to the standard procedure in the following states: Belgium,

Austria, Cyprus, Estonia, Finland, Germany, Ireland, Luxemburg, Slovakia and Slovenia. In the other states – namely, Spain, France, Malta, Netherlands and Portugal – the ESM treaty has been merged with the ratification of Article 136(3) TFEU. In France the combined ratification of the ESM Treaty and Article 136(3) was subject to a fast-track procedure that provided for only one plenary debate. In Greece and Italy national parliaments had to ratify a triple merger: the ESM Treaty, Article 136(3) and the Fiscal Compact.

The ratification procedures of the Fiscal Compact varied significantly across states. The practices observed differed with regard to the degree of national parliaments' involvement or influence. In a number of states voting on particular anti-crisis measures was eliminated: in Cyprus (Fiscal Compact), Greece (EFSF-1), Italy (EFSF-1 and EFSF-2), the Netherlands (EFSF-1) and Portugal (EFSF-2). Plenary debate was entirely eliminated in the following states: Spain (EFSF-1 and EFSF-2), Cyprus (Fiscal Compact), Greece (EFSF-1) and the Netherlands (EFSF-2). In France the number of plenary debates was reduced from three to one (the EFSF-1, EFSF-2, ESM and the Fiscal Compact).

Mergers have taken place in the following states: Spain (ESM and Article 136 TFEU), France (EFSF-1 was merged with the budget bill and the ESM Treaty was merged with Article 136 TFEU), Greece (EFSF-2 was merged with the law on a property tax and bank supervision, the ESM Treaty was merged with Article 136 TFEU and the Fiscal Compact), Italy (Article 136 TFEU, ESM, Fiscal Compact), Malta (ESM merged with Article 136 TFEU), the Netherlands (EFSF-2 with the budgetary law, ESM with Article 136 TFEU) and Portugal (ESM and Article 136 TFEU).

Practices with regard to mergers differed significantly across the states under study. For instance, it was common practice to merge ratification of the ESM Treaty with the revision of Article 136(3) TFEU. Furthermore, the establishment of the EFSF or the increase of its budgetary capacity was merged in a couple of states with domestic budgetary measures. These two instances of mergers do not constitute extreme examples of limitations on national parliaments' powers. In both cases the components of the package were closely related to each other and interdependent. This is to say, financial guarantees provided within the EFSF framework have to be envisaged in the budget. However, other instances of mergers may appear more problematic. For instance, in Greece ratification of the ESM Treaty was merged with the revision of Article 136(3) and ratification of the Fiscal Compact. Furthermore, the balanced budget rule has also been introduced in the national constitution. In Italy, similarly, the ESM Treaty was merged with the revision of Article 136(3) and the Fiscal Compact. Although Italian MPs voted on each component of the package separately, the whole package was debated together, which raises concerns regarding the quality of parliamentary deliberation. In Greece MPs had only one plenary debate and one vote to approve – or reject – the whole legislative package. A further concern is related to the time available for discussion. The qualitative analysis of parliamentary debates in Greece demonstrated that MPs devoted as much attention to procedural aspects as to the very content of the package (Maatsch, 2016). On one hand, the finding demonstrates MPs' awareness of the problem, but on the other, it implies that, due to procedural issues, debate on the content of the legislation was very limited.

The data demonstrate that, first, fast-track procedures and mergers were found in the same states. In other words, parliaments either approved anti-crisis measures with standard procedures or they deviated from that practice. Second, elimination of voting on a particular anti-crisis measure coincided with the elimination of debate. Parliaments in these states basically had no influence over the approval of a given measure. Third, the participation of parliaments was limited most by a combination of fast-track procedures and mergers. In particular, in France the revision of Article 136(3) was merged with ratification of the ESM Treaty. These two measures were approved with a fast-track procedure that reduced the standard number of plenary debates from three to one. That may appear problematic in the French context because implementation of the balanced budget rule has been highly contested. Eventually, in France there was not enough support among the parliamentary parties to incorporate the balanced budget rule into the constitution. Other examples concern states that approved anti-crisis measures with either fast-track procedures or mergers. For instance, in Greece, Italy and Spain the combination of fast-track procedures and mergers either prevented parliamentary debate (and sometimes even voting) or considerably affected the deliberation process by extending the agenda of the plenary debate.

What factors influenced the application of emergency legislation during the reform of European economic governance?

This study identifies four major factors that influenced application of emergency legislation in the member states of the eurozone. Explanatory factors identified at the national level are the domestic constitutional set-up and the attitude of national courts. At the international level the study identified two further factors: economic and political pressure to facilitate the approval process.

At the domestic level, application of fast-track procedures depends, first, on the generosity of the national constitutional set-up and, second, on the attitude of national constitutional or supreme courts. The literature dealing with practices of emergency legislation before the outbreak of the European financial crisis demonstrates that European states differed mostly with regard to the grade of parliaments' exclusion from the legislative process (Cartabia, 2011; Coutts et al., 2015). For instance, whereas in some states emergency legislation makes it possible to limit the standard number of plenary debates, in other states plenary debates can be entirely eliminated. However, before the outbreak of the crisis there was little variation in the horizontal dimension; as a rule, fast-track procedures were applied in extraordinary situations, such as natural disasters or terrorist attacks. In central policy areas, such as employment, emergency legislation constituted a marginal share of standard legislative procedures.

National constitutional and supreme courts played an important role in regulating applications of fast-track procedures (Wendel, 2013; Pernice, 2014). Courts decide whether a particular application of emergency legislation is constitutional or not. As a result, courts enjoy the power to act against limitations of national parliaments' competences in the legislative process.

The most prominent example of national parliaments' empowerment can be found in Germany. The German Constitutional Court has issued four rulings on the institutional reform of European economic governance.[7] In the first ruling on the EFSF and the Economic Adjustment Programme for Greece of 9 July 2011, the Court declared that neither international treaty violates the Basic Law. However, it also stressed that the Bundestag cannot transfer its budgetary powers to other actors. As a consequence, each bailout or increase of budgetary capacity of the EFSF has to be approved by the German parliament (Bundestag). In these respects, the Court's ruling precluded the approval of anti-crisis measures by means of special fast-track procedures that exclude national legislators. The second ruling – of 2 August 2012 – precluded the possibility of delegating powers belonging to the whole parliamentary plenum to a special parliamentary committee that is supposed to decide on urgent matters related to European economic governance. According to the Court, the Bundestag has to exercise its budgetary powers in their entirety. In the third ruling on the ESM and the Euro Plus Pact of 6 March 2012, the Court stated that the government is obliged to inform the German parliament as early as possible regarding all matters related to European economic governance. Finally, in the ruling on the ESM and the Fiscal Compact of 9 December 2012, the Court confirmed that neither the ESM nor the Fiscal Compact violate the constitution (see, for instance, the ruling of the German Constitutional Court of 18 March 2014, BVerfG, 2 BvR 1390/12). However, the parliament has to be consulted on each increase in the ESM budget and on new bailout decisions.

Although some other courts also defended the competences of their national parliaments, no other national parliament has enjoyed such a significant confirmation of its powers as the German Bundestag (Fasone, 2014b). In Austria, for instance, the national parliament acquired the right to vote on every decision related to the ESM. The reform was introduced by a constitutional amendment. Furthermore, the French, Estonian and Finnish parliaments were confirmed in their competence to approve all new financial assistance programmes by voting.

Finally, the most prominent instances of national parliaments' disempowerment could be observed in southern Europe. For instance, in Portugal and Spain the constitutional courts marginalized parliaments vis-à-vis the executive (Fasone, 2014b). In Spain the rulings were particularly controversial because they were based on a different reasoning than the prior rulings on royal decree-law applications from 1982 and 2007. In particular, the recent rulings dismissed the action of unconstitutionality against applications of fast-track procedures (royal decree-law) with regard to both European economic governance and national labour reforms introduced in 2012 (Coutts el al., 2015).

Approval of anti-crisis measures in Spain illustrates very well what concerns can arise from extensive application of fast-track procedures. In the Spanish system we can differentiate ordinary laws from decree-laws. Royal decree-laws are envisaged for extremely urgent situations. The national parliament cannot amend the text of a decree-law unless it transforms it into a legislative scheme dealt with in accordance with the urgent procedure (Article 86 of the Spanish Constitution), which prolongs the procedure somewhat. According to the procedure, a decree-law becomes binding if it is voted by the parliament; a debate is not necessary. If the vote is affirmative, the decree-law becomes an ordinary law. As comparative studies have illustrated (Coutts et al., 2015), while in the pre-crisis period royal decree-laws were rarely applied, in the post-2009 period the royal decree-law has become the major tool for implementing EU legislation related to economic governance. Moreover, in 2012 the number of bills or EU draft legislative acts approved with the royal decree-laws was higher than the number of bills approved as ordinary laws. The predominance of the fast-track procedure generated a discussion on whether such an extensive application of royal decree-laws is justifiable. Among other things, critical voices pointed to the rulings of the Spanish Constitutional Court from 1982 and 2007 in which the Court stated explicitly that governments should not apply royal decree-laws for structural issues or policies.[8] In other southern European states where numerous fast-track measures were applied, supreme or constitutional courts did not rule that their application is unconstitutional. As a result, national parliaments' powers were not actively defended.

In sum, most supreme or constitutional courts in the eurozone have not assumed an active role of parliaments' defenders. Particularly the position of southern European courts has contributed to diminishing the role of national parliaments in states that were most directly affected by the new legislative measures.

Finally, governments' decision to limit parliaments' powers has been also influenced by international factors. The European financial crisis contributed to generating an asymmetry in the substantive equality of debtor states. According to Article 4(2) TEU, all member states and their self-governing institutions enjoy equal status: 'The Union shall respect the equality of Member States before the Treaties as well as their national identities, inherent in their fundamental structures, political and constitutional, inclusive of regional and local self-government.' However, although all EU member states enjoy equal status de jure, they are not automatically unrestricted in the exercise of their formal powers (Maduro, 2012). Hence, the substantive equality of southern European states became restricted when they accepted bailout loans.

The peculiarity of the eurozone crisis is that two types of actors became entitled to decide on budgetary matters of debtor states: non-elected institutions (the International Monetary Fund [IMF] and the European Central Bank)[9] and national political actors (governments and parliaments of other eurozone states). Before the monetary union was established, European states applying for a loan from the IMF also had to accept some conditionalities. However, the process was not politicized to the same extent. In the eurozone the establishment of the EFSF and the increase in its budgetary capacity depended on national governments' and parliaments' unanimous consent. As a consequence, a veto by one national parliament meant that eurozone states facing liquidity problems could not obtain a bailout.

In the economic dimension, exposure to external conditionality in national budgetary matters had a negative effect on national sovereign powers. National parliaments, responsible for tailoring national budgets, were most directly affected by restrictions in that area. Every bailout loan has been accompanied by the so-called Memorandum of Understanding (MoU) that stipulates the reforms that have to be undertaken by states under the programme. Oversight of the Memorandum's implementation has been conducted by an external body, the so-called 'Troika' composed of the European Commission, the European Central Bank and the International Monetary Fund. Furthermore, exposure to national conditionality also enabled foreign political institutions to review the national budgetary plans of bailout states. In a now famous example, the German Bundestag reviewed and debated the Irish budget before the Dáil (Irish parliament) had done so.

In the political dimension, the acquisition of bailout loans has also been conditioned on completing ratification of the Fiscal Compact and introducing the balanced budget rule into domestic legislation. That condition has also constrained national parliaments in exercising their powers: practically speaking, parliaments in bailout states could neither reject the Fiscal Compact nor delay the ratification process. Otherwise they risked losing financial aid. Against that background, governments in southern European states had a strong incentive to minimize the likelihood of failure to approve anti-crisis measures, for instance by limiting national parliaments' powers.

Conclusions

This chapter has analyzed how the intergovernmental reform process of European economic governance affected oversight practices of national parliaments in that policy area. In particular, the analysis examined which national parliaments became disempowered in that process and which factors contributed to that. The analysis provides information on how all national parliaments in the eurozone were involved in the approval of the following anti-crisis measures: the European Financial Stability Facility (EFSF) – both its establishment and the increase of its budgetary capacity – the European Stability Mechanism (ESM) and the Treaty on Stability, Coordination and Governance in the Economic and Monetary Union.

Disempowerment of national parliaments manifested itself through extensive application of so-called emergency legislation. These procedures, codified in every democratic state, made it possible to accelerate the legislative process and reduce the risk of a failure to ratify by limiting national parliaments' involvement. Emergency legislation limits national parliaments' powers to a different extent: whereas in some states only the number of plenary debates is reduced, in other states plenary debates and voting can be eliminated entirely.

In the first step, the analysis mapped in which states national parliaments' powers were limited – and to what extent. In the second step, the chapter examined which domestic and international factors influenced application of emergency legislation. These factors were: domestic constitutional set-up, constitutional or supreme courts' activity and international political and economic pressure.

The comparative analysis demonstrated that southern European states were far more disempowered than northern European states. Although all states envisage various forms of emergency legislation, these procedures were employed first and foremost in southern Europe. National constitutional and supreme courts played a very important role in that process. In southern Europe courts issued rulings that supported national governments' extensive application of emergency legislation. For instance, in Spain acts approved with emergency procedures outnumbered acts approved with the standard procedure. Furthermore, emergency legislation has been extended to policy areas that initially were reformed only with standard procedures, such as public policy. No court in southern Europe declared these practices to be unconstitutional. In northern Europe, by contrast, many constitutional courts confirmed or fostered national parliaments' competences in European economic governance, the most prominent case being Germany. Finally, parliaments in southern European states we also disempowered due to international economic and political pressure. For instance, acquisition of bailout loans was conditioned on ratification of the Fiscal Compact.

From a normative perspective it can be argued that the legitimacy of European economic governance clearly suffered due to the disempowerment of national parliaments during the reform process. Not surprisingly, many scholars advocated fostering EMU's legitimacy by re-empowering national parliaments along the lines of the Lisbon process (Kröger and Bellamy, 2016). However, the question remains whether re-empowerment of national parliaments would be sufficient to meet the normative requirements of democratic accountability in that policy area. The findings of this chapter suggest a negative answer.

First, at the European level, national parliaments' role predominantly concerns control of governments' actions. It is the European Parliament, not national parliaments, that is involved by means of the ordinary legislative procedure in all subsequent stages of the law-making process. As a consequence, democratic accountability within European economic governance also depends on the European Parliament's formal competences and its de facto performance in the legislative process. If the formal powers of the European Parliament are limited – as was the case, for example, during the approval of the temporary bailout fund – the democratic accountability of economic governance is also negatively affected.

Second, the analysis demonstrated that national parliaments in the eurozone do not exercise equal oversight powers at the EU level. The discrepancies in parliaments' powers have their roots in national constitutional set-ups but also in parliaments' relations with the executive or national courts. In particular, parliaments that enjoy stronger constitutional powers can conduct their oversight more efficiently. However, national parliaments' powers can be limited by governments and courts on a short-term basis. Furthermore, international pressure exerted on governments can also rapidly worsen the conditions for parliamentary oversight. As a consequence, if some parliaments are empowered and others disempowered, such asymmetry of control powers has a negative impact on the quality of democratic control in the EU. This is because some parliaments enjoy a privileged position in controlling decision-making at the EU level, whereas others remain disadvantaged in that process. Therefore, the condition for equality of national representative institutions guaranteed by the Treaty is fulfilled only *de jure* but not *de facto*: national parliaments are not equal in the exercise of their oversight competences at the EU level.

Therefore, the findings of this chapter suggest that oversight of European policy-making should be actively fostered at three different levels: national parliaments and the European Parliament and possibly also at the transnational interparliamentary level (Cooper, 2014). The newly established Interparliamentary Conference on Stability, Economic Coordination and Governance in the European Union provides an opportunity for national parliaments to exchange opinions and conduct collective oversight – and on equal footing – of current European economic matters. Further research should, therefore, concentrate on examining how effectively national parliaments use the available vertical and horizontal channels in their oversight practice. There is a clear need to conduct in-depth case-studies, particularly investigating practices of national parliaments that were classified as outliers in this comparative study.

Notes

1 The database was compiled by three researchers who covered particular states according to their personal language skills: Athena Charalamboglou (Greece), Dr. Patricio Galella (compilation of the database as well as general legal expertise) and Dr. Aleksandra Maatsch (design and compilation of the database).
2 Regarding management of the European Stability Mechanism see Fasone (2014b).
3 House of Lords. (2009). *Fast-Track Legislation: Constitutional Implications and Safeguards* (London: The Stationery Office).
4 Ibid., page 15.
5 Ibid.
6 According to procedure, the Italian parliament converted the decree into a law and then voted on its enactment.
7 BVerfG 09/07/2011, BVerfG 02/28/2012, BVerfG 06/3ß/2012, BVerfG 09/12/2012.
8 Sentencia del Tribunal Constitucional 29/1982, Sentencia del Tribunal Constitucional 68/2007.
9 To some extent also the European Commission.

4 Drivers of political parties' voting behaviour in European economic governance

The ultimate decline of the economic cleavage?

Introduction

Since the outbreak of the European financial crisis national parliamentary parties have been involved in approving the new legal and policy measures reforming European economic governance. The new role has been particularly challenging for national parties. On one hand, parliamentary parties, being responsible for tailoring national budgets, possess considerable fiscal policy expertise. Furthermore, financial crises are by no means new for parties: since the Second World War European economies have been regularly confronted with currency or asset prices crises. On the other hand, the introduction of a common currency (euro) radically changed the initial scope conditions. First, members of the eurozone were limited in their choice of anti-crisis policies: for instance, governments were no longer free to devaluate. Second, the crisis generated a profound tension between the domestic demands of national constituencies and international interdependence of decision-makers; that is, in many states the preferences of voters collided with the anti-crisis approach agreed by governments of the eurozone. The crisis also antagonized northern and southern European states giving rise to a new conflict between 'surplus' and 'deficit' eurozone states. Against that background, the general question emerges: to what extent has parliamentary parties' voting behaviour on anti-crisis measures been affected by the new economic and institutional conditions? In particular, which factors account for national parliamentary parties' vote outcomes on the major legislative measures reforming European economic governance? What are the major conflict lines among the analyzed parties? Are the established patterns of political parties' voting behaviour confirmed or disconfirmed by the new empirical data?

According to the literature, political parties in democratic states fulfil two basic functions: they represent their voters and implement policies. The first function of political parties has been conceptualized as responsiveness

(Mair, 2009; Bardi et al., 2014), meaning that citizens, by voting for a given party, select representatives who are expected to implement policies in accordance with their interests (Hibbing and Theiss-Morse, 2001). The second function of political parties, often referred to as responsibility, is associated with governing (Mair, 2009). Responsibility implies that parties respect international obligations vis-à-vis regional organizations or international markets (Bardi et al., 2014) but also take into account the long-term needs of their state that are rarely voiced directly by their voters, such as national security concerns.

A political system can be recognized as legitimate as long as political parties perform well their two basic functions. Namely, the two dimensions of legitimacy, input and output legitimacy (Scharpf, 2009) are closely linked to responsiveness and responsibility. Whereas output legitimacy concerns the performance of institutions in delivering policy outputs, input legitimacy denotes conditions for the democratic self-government and electoral accountability of governors. Therefore, a political system is legitimate if it fulfils the following conditions: political parties represent their voters' interests organized along the main cleavages (responsiveness), governments and political parties remain accountable for their actions (responsiveness) and governments and political parties deliver policy outputs which satisfy their voters and respect international agreements (responsibility).

Recently, scholars have observed that the new circumstances generated by the sovereign debt crisis in the eurozone are likely to affect the responsiveness and responsibility of political parties (Bohle, 2014; Maatsch, 2014; Rose, 2014). In particular, the literature has observed that governing parties in bailout (debtor) states are more likely to prioritize international obligations vis-à-vis international markets than governing parties in creditor states (Bohle, 2014). This is because governments facing liquidity or solvency problems have to accept conditionalities accompanying a bailout loan: membership of the monetary union precluded alternative options, such as devaluation. By the same token, national parliamentary parties gave up sovereignty in the central area of their political activity, namely, the national budget. Parties in bailout states demonstrated that they are very much aware of the dilemma, as one Irish MP observed:

> This country is fighting to get its sovereignty back, but the reality is that the future of Europe requires greater economic integration. We know the political reality that greater integration with a reduction in sovereignty may not be acceptable to the people.[1]

On the other hand, societies of northern European creditor states also voiced criticisms. In particular, many voters disapproved of financial solidarity measures among the member states of the eurozone. However, governments of creditor states, uncertain about the possible spillover of the crisis into their own states, and particularly into their banking systems (Thompson, 2013), had to provide financial guarantees to debtor states within the bailout fund. However, the driving motivation of political parties in creditor states was not solidarity but rather the national economic interest (Closa and Maatsch, 2014).

Although the literature on parliamentary parties' behaviour in the European sovereign debt crisis is quickly growing, most published contributions have provided a fragmented picture. For instance, studies have often concentrated on the analysis of a single anti-crisis measure (Closa and Maatsch, 2014). Other studies have focussed only on a limited number of eurozone states (Wendler, 2014; De Giorgi and Moury, 2015) or exclusively on governing parties (Bohle, 2014). Finally, there are also studies which concentrate exclusively on the impact of formal competences on parliamentary parties' behaviour (Fasone, 2014a). Against that background, the fragmented empirical evidence does not allow us to reach any general conclusions about the drivers of parliamentary parties' behaviour in the reform of European economic governance. This chapter aims to fill that gap by analyzing how national parliamentary parties in eurozone states[2] voted on the subsequent anti-crisis measures: the European Financial Stability Facility (EFSF) (establishment of the fund and increase of its budgetary capacity), the European Stability Mechanism (ESM) and the Treaty on Stability, Coordination and Governance in the Economic and Monetary Union (TSCG) also referred to as the Fiscal Compact. Although all the above mentioned measures belong to the so-called 'reform package', their content differs substantially. The EFSF and the ESM established a bailout found providing financial support to eurozone member states which could no longer finance themselves on the markets (due to liquidity or solvency problems). While the EFSF was established as a temporary solution, the ESM became a permanent bailout fund. The Fiscal Compact is a stricter version of the previous Stability and Growth Pact. Member states bound by the treaty are required to introduce into domestic law a self-correcting mechanism which shall guarantee that their national budgets are balanced. In particular, the general budget deficit shall not exceed 3 percent of GDP, the structural deficit shall be less than 1 percent of GDP and the debt-to-GDP ratio shall remain below 60 percent.

In the empirical dimension, the chapter tests the extent to which the vote outcome can be explained by the following factors: (1) international interdependence, (2) response to voters' preferences, (3) institutional cleavage (government-opposition), (4) economic policy preferences, (5) party's position on the EU, (6) conflict between creditors and debtors and (7) formal approval procedures. The empirical analysis is conducted with help of the statistical binary logit model; the unit of the analysis is defined as the vote of a particular party on a given anti-crisis measure.

The analysis demonstrated that governing parties, irrespective of their policy preferences or bailout status, voted in favour of anti-crisis measures. That finding clearly confirmed the power of international interdependence in decision-making on European economic governance. In contrast, opposition parties voted either in favour or against. The decisive factor explaining opposition parties' vote outcome has been their position on the EU. In particular, opposition parties that voted against anti-crisis measures were Eurosceptic. Furthermore, whereas negative votes among opposition parties were less likely the higher the 'trust of the population in its government' and the trust in the problem-solving capacity of the EU, the likelihood of no-votes increased with the level of trust in national parliaments. Interestingly, opposition parties' policy preferences measured on the economic left–right scale do not seem to have any significant impact. Furthermore, an additional test measuring the impact of extreme left–right positions on the vote outcome did not produce significant results either.

This chapter begins by discussing the literature and hypotheses explaining national parliamentary parties' voting patterns on European issues. The next section presents the legal status of the European anti-crisis measures and explains how they were approved by national legislators. Finally, after a short presentation of the methodological approach, the chapter engages with empirical findings. The last sections (discussion and conclusions) evaluate the empirical and normative implications of findings and suggest directions for further research.

What factors explain political parties' voting patterns on European anti-crisis measures? Literature review and hypotheses

The literature on political parties identifies the following factors as possibly accounting for political parties' vote outcomes on the European anti-crisis measures: international obligations (Bohle, 2014; Rose, 2014), domestic voters' preferences (Downs, 1957; Dalton, 1985; Ezrow et al., 2010), party positions on redistribution (Alesina and Rosenthal, 1995; Boix, 2000; Broz, 2013; Closa and Maatsch, 2014; Maatsch, 2014), position on European integration (Hooghe and Marks, 2008; Szczerbiak and Taggart, 2008 and 2013), impact of bailout loans (Bohle, 2014; Maatsch, 2014) and formal approval procedures (Coutts et al., 2015, Maatsch, 2015).

The first hypothesis tested in this chapter stipulates that *due to the presence of international obligations, governing parties in both creditor and debtor states vote in favour of anti-crisis measures.* Responsibility towards international obligations is foremost a feature of governing, not opposition, parties. According to Birch (1964) and Mair (2011) responsibility of governing parties implies prudence, consistency and predictability in their actions over a longer period of time as well as a sense of duty to respect international norms and commitments that have been made by previous governments. In other words, there is an expectation that democratic governments, as representatives of their states at the international area, shall respect existing international agreements even if they are not entirely in favour of them.

The European financial crisis has demonstrated that prioritization of international responsibility by decision-makers very often stands in conflict to the principles of sovereignty and democracy. According to Rodrik (2011), global economic integration generated a profound tension between the principles of democracy, sovereignty and economic integration. This tension has been carried to extremes by the financial crisis in Europe.

The interdependence of national economies in the eurozone is particularly strong. First, membership of the monetary union has an impact on states' financial position on the markets. When the common currency was introduced, peripheral states could borrow more cheaply on international markets, benefiting from lower interest rates. As some economists observed (de Grauwe and Ji, 2012), financial markets underpriced the risk before the crisis and overpriced it during the crisis. As a consequence, governments were under pressure to overcome domestic opposition. They were aware that a failure to ratify in one state could put the whole reform process on hold, which could have profound economic consequences for all members of the eurozone. The task proved to be particularly difficult to governments in bailout states that committed themselves to anti-crisis legislation even though these measures limited their sovereignty and became contested by the voters.

Finally, the literature on political parties stresses the impact of the very close link between governments and parliamentary majorities on decision-making processes. First, the literature notes that governing parties rarely vote against measures approved by their governments (Raunio, 2009). On the contrary, they seek to legitimize their government's decision. That mechanism is related to the fact that the major cleavage in domestic politics is between government and opposition and not between government and national parliament. Secondly, given the intergovernmental and technocratic form in which the anti-crisis measures were negotiated, governing parties were more likely to identify with them than the opposition parties.

In contrast to governing parties, opposition parties are not constrained by international obligations: they could respond to the preferences of their constituencies (as a vote- or office-seeking strategy) or vote according to their ideological position. The by now classic spatial electoral models demonstrate that parties, in order to get re-elected, tend to address the short-term interests of the median voter (general electorate model) (Downs, 1957) or the interests of the mean party supporter (partisan constituency model) (Dalton, 1985; Ezrow et al., 2010). Ratification of anti-crisis measures provided a particular opportunity for opposition parties to vote *responsively*, particularly if governing parties disregarded their voters' opinions. Therefore, according to the second hypotheses tested in this chapter, *opposition parties are more likely to vote responsively the higher the public discontent with the reform process.*

The literature demonstrates that parties' behaviour is also influenced by ideology (Cranston and Mair, 1980). As parties adhere to certain ideologies in a path-dependent manner, it is possible to predict parties' behaviour on that basis. According to the literature, parties opt for macroeconomic measures which coincide with their general economic ideology: parties located on the economic 'right' opt for neoliberal measures, whereas parties located on the economic 'left' advocate 'Keynesian' ones (Alesina and Rosenthal, 1995; Boix, 2000).

The literature notes that while the conflict over redistribution is present at the European level, it differs to some extent from the conflict over national policies (Hooghe and Marks, 2008). While in nation–states redistribution takes place at the individual level (from the richer to the poorer citizens), in the EU redistribution has a national dimension (from the wealthier to poorer states). As the literature notes, the willingness to redistribute is higher if recipients are perceived as members of the same community. Therefore, pursuit of redistribution between states is likely to encounter more contestation than within one state.

More recent literature focussing on the financial crisis (Broz, 2013) also demonstrates that a response – like the run-up – to a crisis is also likely to be informed by the economic ideology of the governing political party. In particular, political parties representing the right-wing of the economic spectrum are likely to advocate pro-cyclical measures, such as so-called 'austerity' policies. In contrast, parties representing the economic left are more likely to propose anti-cyclical measures, for instance, increases in government spending. In general, given the fact that the European anti-crisis measures are based on pro-cyclical 'austerity' policies, *it can be expected that opposition parties representing the economic 'right' (both in debtor and creditor states) support these measures to a greater extent than parties located on the economic 'left'.*

However, it is also likely that the influence of the economic ideology varies across different anti-crisis measures. On one hand, as the right-wing parties are less sympathetic towards redistribution, they may be more likely to vote against the EFSF and the ESM than the left-wing parties. On the other hand, right-wing parties may be more willing to vote in favour of the Fiscal Compact, for it strengthens the budgetary surveillance and makes it difficult to pursue interventionist politics. In order to test that, the quantitative analysis investigates the impact of economic ideology along each particular measure.

According to the fourth hypothesis tested in this chapter, *Eurosceptic opposition parties are more likely to vote against anti-crisis measures than pro-European parties*. As many authors have noted (Szczerbiak and Taggart, 2008 and 2013), parties classified as Eurosceptic object in principle to any and all initiatives that might assign more competences to Brussels. Two aspects of the reform are likely to be contested by Eurosceptic parties: establishment of the bailout fund and closer surveillance of national budgetary politics by the European Council and the European Commission. On one hand, Eurosceptics in debtor states are likely to disapprove their partial loss of sovereignty related to entering a bailout programme. Namely, in bailout states budgetary policy is no longer exclusively controlled by the executive and legislature, but also by the so-called 'Troika' composed of the European Commission, the European Central Bank and the International Monetary Fund, which supervises compliance with the Memoranda of Understanding. On the other hand, although creditor states remain sovereign in their national budgetary politics, they provide financial guarantees to states that received a loan from the bailout fund. If bailout states fail to service their debt, creditor states are obliged to pay their share. Hence, it is very likely that Eurosceptic parties in creditor states will also take a negative stance. Finally, it can also be expected that closer surveillance of national budgets by the Council and the Commission will be contested by Eurosceptic parties.

In the literature we find an argument that the introduction of bailout loans had an impact on political parties' behaviour (Maatsch, 2014). Bailout programmes generated a conflict between northern and southern European states. Whereas in debtor states the resentment was fuelled by the disapproval of austerity measures and loss of national sovereignty, the antagonism in creditor states was generated by anti-solidaristic attitudes (Closa and Maatsch, 2014). The resentment evoked by the bailout has not crosscut with any pre-existing political division; rather, it has manifested itself within parties representing the economic left, right, pro- and anti-European positions. As a consequence, the bailout conflict can be associated rather with the national level. Against that background, *if the contestation of anti-crisis measures is explained by the bailout conflict, the votes against are likely to be observed across different ideological positions of parties in both creditor and debtor states*.

Finally, it has been observed that specific voting procedures in parliaments (for instance, simple versus special majorities) also influence vote outcomes. Various empirical studies have demonstrated that there was a significant divergence in approval procedures of anti-crisis measures (Benz, 2013; Coutts et al., 2015; Fasone, 2014b, Maatsch, 2015). In particular, in bailout states governments introduced various institutional arrangements which allowed approving anti-crisis measures with a minimized risk of defection. In contrast, in creditor states anti-crisis measures were approved predominantly with standard procedures.

The factors which mostly disempowered national parliament in southern European states were: the legislation of emergency (fast-track procedures and mergers), national constitutional or supreme courts' activity and the loss of substantial equality by parliaments. Fast-track procedures are codified in each European state; their major goal is to accelerate the legislative process in unusual circumstances. Fast-track arrangements differ from state to state: they can concern limitation in the number of plenary debates (i.e. from three to one) but also elimination of voting (Maatsch, 2015). Mergers constitute legislative packages composed of two or more legal acts which usually have to be debated together and approved with one vote, which seriously limits the impact of parliaments. According to the literature, courts' rulings have rather disempowered national parliaments in bailout states[3] and empowered selected parliaments in creditor states (predominantly the Bundestag). Finally, acquisition of a bailout loan was often conditioned on approval of specific anti-crisis measures (i.e. the Fiscal Compact). That factor limited parliaments in bailout states in their sovereign exercise of formal powers (hence, limitation of substantial equality). According to the literature, states which approved all anti-crisis measures by means of standard procedures were: Belgium, Austria, Estonia, Finland, Germany, Ireland, Luxemburg, Slovakia and Slovenia (Fasone, 2014b; Coutts et al., 2015; Maatsch, 2015). States which applied fast-track procedures or mergers were: Spain, France, Cyprus, Greece, Italy, Malta, Netherlands and Portugal. As a consequence, if vote outcome is explained by differences in voting procedures, the variation is to be observed at the country-level. Hence, *parliamentary parties in bailout states are less likely to vote against anti-crisis measures than parliamentary parties in creditor states.*

Research design, methodological approach and the database used in this study

The empirical data on the dependent variable (vote outcome by party) have been obtained from the internet pages of national parliaments. All national parliaments publish their vote outcomes, though the form in which the data is presented, as well as the grade of detail, may differ. In particular, some parliaments publish detailed name-lists; others only provide data on how each parliamentary party voted. Furthermore, whereas some parliaments publish vote outcomes together with minutes from plenary sessions during which the voting took place, others provide vote outcomes in separate documents. Due to these discrepancies it was sometimes necessary to enquire directly at national parliaments in order to establish how the official information can be accessed.

Explanatory variables were obtained from three different sources. The data on lending operations (bailouts) were obtained from the internet pages of the European Financial Stability Facility[4] and the European Stability Mechanism.[5] The data on trust in institutions and evaluation of their effectiveness in combating the crisis were obtained from Eurobarometer surveys 73, 74, 75, 76 and 77. Finally, political parties' positions regarding the European integration as well as economic preferences were extracted from the PIREDEU database. The first limitation of the source was that PIREDEU does not provide information on small (often regional) parties which are usually poorly represented at the national level (one or two seats). Second, the database has not covered political parties which were established shortly before the analyzed votes. As a consequence, a number of observations had to be excluded from the analysis.

In the analytical model the vote outcome on a given measure was matched with the corresponding results of the Eurobarometer survey. The analysis covered almost all states of the eurozone, namely, Austria, Belgium, Estonia, Finland, France, Germany, Greece, Ireland, Italy, Luxemburg, Malta, Netherlands, Portugal, Slovakia, Slovenia and Spain.[6]

In total, the sample consists of 383 votes. Due to missing values in the PIREDEU dataset, the data used for the regression analysis had to be reduced to 264 observations. An observation has been defined as one vote of a particular party on a given measure (or bundle of measures). In the 16 countries included in the sample, a total of 58 votes have been analyzed. The dependent variable has been operationalized as the majority vote outcome of a given party on a given measure.

In order to test the hypotheses, a set of different regression models has been run on the dataset. First, it turned out that none of the governing parties in the sample voted against any of the measures.[7] Therefore, the variable 'government party' by itself could already explain 113 positive outcomes. The sample was, hence, reduced to opposition parties. Second, the data plot shows that 332 out of 383 party votes were unanimous so that a discrete model was preferred over a logistic regression. In the dataset covering only opposition parties the dependent variable was defined as 'majority against'.

The following independent variables were tested in different model layouts:

Party-related variables:

- position_EU (positive or negative attitude towards EU according to PIREDEU)
- position_leftright (according to PIREDEU scale)
- position_extreme (created from PIREDEU; distance from political centre)

Country-related variables:

- bailout state (dummy variable)
- fast track (simplified parliamentary procedure)
- unemployment (Eurostat)
- trust_national government (Eurobarometer)
- trust_national parliament (Eurobarometer)
- trust_EU (Eurobarometer)
- effective_EU (Eurobarometer)
- effective_natgov (Eurobarometer)

Content-related variables:

- EFSF-1 (dummy variable)
- EFSF-2 (dummy variable)
- Fiscal Compact (dummy variable)
- ESM (dummy variable)

Constructed variable:

- bailout × leftright (bailout = −1 and non-bailout = 1; left = negative, right = positive)

Based on the PIREDEU classification of parties on the left–right axis, the impact of the economic stance of the parties on their voting behaviour was tested. Next to the standard PIREDEU left–right variable, an 'extreme position' variable was created measuring the distance from the political centre. The idea behind this second variable was that the correlation with the vote outcome could be u-shaped or v-shaped, with parties both on the extreme left and on the extreme right voting more regularly against the measures.

Another variant of the PIREDEU classification was a multiplication with the bailout variable (in this case 1 for non-bailout states and −1 for bailout states). On the one hand, it was likely that right-wing parties in wealthier countries would be reluctant to support the analyzed measures due to their economic stance and their national economic interests. On the other hand, left-wing parties in bailout states could have rejected the analyzed measures also due to their ideological stance and their national economic interests. However, none of the left–right variables were significant. By contrast, the 'pro-EU' variable was highly significant in all of the models.

Empirical findings

The following variables turned out to be significant in the model with the best fit: 'pro-Europeanness' of the party according to PIREDEU (fewer refusals), trust of the population in its government (fewer refusals), trust of the population in its parliaments (more refusals) and positive evaluation of the EU's effectiveness with regard to the combat of the crisis (fewer refusals). Though the model can only partially explain the vote outcomes, the strong significance of the 'pro-EU' variable and the missing impact of left–right cleavages are robust results.

The empirical findings confirm the first hypothesis: almost all governing parties voted in favour of anti-crisis measures throughout the whole period, irrespective of the measure in question, level of social contestation or presence of financial assistance programme in their state. Therefore, the variable 'government party' could already explain 113 out of 207 positive outcomes. Furthermore, almost all governing parties voted unanimously in favour: there were no internal splinter groups voting against anti-crisis measures. There was also no change over time or across different anti-crisis measures. Namely, governing parties have not voted differently on the bailout fund and the Fiscal Compact.

In the second step, the analyzed sample was narrowed down to opposition parties in order to investigate which factors account for their vote outcome. According to the hypotheses tested in this chapter, opposition parties are free from international obligations and, hence, their vote on anti-crisis measures can be informed by different factors. The explanatory model tested whether opposition parties' vote outcomes corresponded to (1) their voters' preferences, (2) general macroeconomic preferences of political parties (3) political parties' positions on European integration, (4) presence of a financial assistance programme and (5) formal approval procedures. The analysis demonstrated that opposition parties' voting behaviour could be explained by the following factors: political parties' position on European integration, public trust in national governments and in national parliaments. Other variables tested in this study did not turn out to be significant.

As expected, opposition parties demonstrated an entirely different pattern of voting behaviour from governing parties. In roughly 38 percent of the votes, the party majority voted against the measures. Hence, the goal of the second step in the analysis was to establish which opposition parties voted in favour and which voted against. Out of various regression models which were tested for this study, a binary logit model was selected as the reference model based on model test statistics. In that model the dependent variable has been operationalized as 'majority of parliamentarians within a political party voted against'. The model correctly predicts 138 out of 151 cases. Together with the 113 positive votes by government parties, the two-step model can explain 251 out of 274 cases, or 92 percent.

The variable measuring support for European integration was highly significant in all models. The finding demonstrates that parties voted on anti-crisis measures according to their position on European integration. In particular, pro-EU parties supported the analyzed anti-crisis measures whereas Eurosceptic parties opposed them. That trend was observed both in creditor and debtor states.

Interestingly, three variables created from Eurobarometer results turned out to have a significant impact. In countries where the public trust in the national government has been high, the measures negotiated at the EU level were also more often supported by the opposition parties. By contrast, in

Table 4.1 Explanatory factors, party vote outcome on European anti-crisis measures

Independent variables	Coefficient	Standard deviation	z value	p value
constant	**+1,97**	0,982	+2,00	0,045**
Party: *Positive perception of EU*	**-0,20**	0,068	-2,93	*0,003***
Population: *Trust in national government*	**-0,10**	0,046	-2,16	*0,031***
Trust in national parliament(s)	**+0,14**	0,055	+2,60	*0,009****
EU problem-solving capacity	**-0,10**	0,046	-2,10	*0,036***
McFadden's R^2	0,46	Akaike (AIC)		119,0
Corrected R^2	0,41	Schwartz		134,1
Log likelihood	54,5	Hannan-Quinn		125,1

* significant at the 10% level
** significant at the 5% level
*** significant at the 1% level
$N = 151$; country-level clustered standard errors variables selection based on test statistics

Source: Author analysis

countries where the level of trust in national parliaments was high, opposition parties were more likely to vote against the analyzed measures. Finally, in countries where the population perceived the EU as effective in combating the crisis support for the measures was also higher in parliament.

The fixed effects of the different measures were not significant in the reference model, meaning that the parties' voting behaviour did not change significantly over time. Opposition parties seemed to vote on the subsequent measures applying the same criteria, even though both the content and the legal status of the measures differed significantly.

Furthermore, the economic cleavage (left–right) was not significant for the vote outcome in any of the tested models. Surprisingly, vote outcomes on the reform process of the European economic governance were not related to the basic macroeconomic positions of political parties. An alternative variable was created in order to test whether extreme economic positions (extreme left or extreme right) had an impact on the vote outcome. Here the expectation was that the relation with the vote outcome could be u-shaped or v-shaped, with parties both on the extreme left and on the extreme right voting more regularly against the measures. However, that was not the case. The differences in parties' vote outcome could not be attributed to economic positions, even the extreme ones. As a consequence, economic positions of parties were irrelevant for the vote outcome on anti-crisis measures. Finally, none of the country-level variables investigating whether vote outcomes correlated with the presence of a bailout loan or particular ratification procedure proved to be significant.

The qualitative analysis of voting behaviour among independent (unaffiliated) MPs did not yield a pattern; that is, they voted both in favour of and against the anti-crisis measures. Independent (unaffiliated) MPs usually constitute a small share of all national MPs, approximately 1 percent or less. However, in some bailout states their number has increased in recent years. In Greece the share even grew to almost 10 percent as Greek MPs have begun to abandon their mainstream parties in protest.

Discussion and conclusions

The chapter analyzed national parties' vote outcomes on the major anti-crisis measures reforming the European economic governance, namely the European Financial Stability Facility (EFSF) (both the establishment of the fund and the increase of its budgetary capacity), the European Stability Mechanism (ESM) and the Fiscal Compact. The analysis covered all eurozone members,[8] with exception of two states. The unit of the analysis was defined as a vote by a party on a particular measure. The sample comprises 402 observations. The empirical analysis was based on a set of logit models testing the impact of the following factors: governing status, the economic left–right cleavage, position on EU integration, impact of public opinion (measured by trust in national and EU institutions and evaluation of their crisis-solving capacity), the impact of the conflict between debtor and creditor states as well as the impact of formal ratification procedures.

The chapter demonstrates that the voting pattern of governing and opposition parties reflects an entirely different pattern. Whereas none of the governing parties in the sample voted against the analyzed anti-crisis measures, opposition parties voted in favour or against. As expected, the support of governing parties was driven by the international responsibility to continue reforms of the European economic governance as well as the awareness of interdependence of states in the eurozone. In particular, given the fact that the analyzed anti-crisis measures required the unanimous approval of all states (or 'special' majorities), governing parties were aware that a failure to ratify by their state could put the whole reform process on hold.

In the light of recent developments in several European states, it has to be noted that during the period of the analysis, there were no radical left, radical right or TAN governments. Therefore, we do not know whether these parties would also support anti-crisis measures on the grounds of international responsibility.[9]

The major factor explaining opposition parties' vote outcomes across all model formulations was their position on the EU. In particular, Eurosceptic opposition parties opposed anti-crisis measures whereas pro-EU opposition parties supported them. As a consequence, opposition parties have not differentiated between the ratification of the bailout fund and the Fiscal Compact even though the content of the two measures could be evaluated differently by the left-wing and right-wing parties. That finding demonstrates that opposition parties' position on anti-crisis measures boiled down to the basic question whether a given party supported the European integration project or not.

Furthermore, opposition parties' vote outcome has been fairly responsive towards voters' preferences. In particular, in states where voters' trust in their governments was high, opposition parties were more likely to vote in favour of all analyzed anti-crisis measures. On the contrary, opposition parties were more prone to vote against anti-crisis measures if voters' trust in national parliaments was high. Finally, the analysis also demonstrated that the higher the public trust in the capacity of the EU to solve the financial crisis, the more likely were the opposition parties to vote in favour of anti-crisis measures. How to interpret these findings? Primarily, if voters believe that governments, but also the EU, represent properly their interests, opposition parties are also more likely to demonstrate their consent towards the anti-crisis politics. In other words, the more the voters were satisfied with the output legitimacy (performance of national or EU institutions in delivering satisfactory policy outputs), the more likely were the opposition parties to support anti-crisis measures. However, if voters declare that they trust predominantly in national parliaments, opposition parties are more prone to vote against anti-crisis measures. It particular, high public trust in national parliaments signals that voters do not only trust the ruling majority but also – or rather – opposition parties. Hence, high trust in parliaments suggests that alternative policy-proposals are also recognized as legitimate by the voters. That encourages opposition parties to challenge the governing majority.

Probably the most surprising finding is the irrelevance of the left–right cleavage for the vote outcome. The model also tested the impact of the radical left and right positions, but these proved to be irrelevant. Furthermore, the growing public discontent with the reform of EU economic governance was not reflected in the vote outcomes. Rather, the data suggest a disconnection between the parties' vote outcomes and their voters' preferences. Finally, the majority of governing and opposition parties reached an internal consensus on anti-crisis measures and voted unanimously in favour or against them. The finding confirms that the analyzed parties managed to present unitary positions even in a highly controversial policy area such as European economic governance.

The implications of the findings presented in this chapter go beyond the approval of anti-crisis measures. In the literature, national parliamentary parties were recognized to play an important role in *domesticating* and *normalizing* EU policy-making. According to Kröger and Bellamy (2016: 4):

> The politicisation of EU affairs need not be equated with Euroscepticism and the rise of populist movements. Rather, by debating EU matters more fully within national parliaments, parties can reconnect EU policy to domestic democratic processes and the normal political cleavages of left and right.

However, this chapter demonstrates that national parliamentary parties failed to incorporate the economic dimension in decisions on European economic governance; namely, parties' voting patterns were predominantly explained with their position on the European Union. The finding appears surprising given that probably no other policy area is so closely related to the question of redistribution. By the same token, this chapter confirms the thesis according to which political parties' preferences are rather structured by the conflict over identity than redistribution (Hooghe and Marks, 2008).

Parliamentary parties failed to reconnect nationally-delineated conflict lines with the decision-making on European economic governance. As Hix and Noury (2009) demonstrated, national conflict lines with regard to EU

Table 4.2 Regression models on vote outcomes

Model type	Country variables				Selected			
Indep. variables	All							
Parameter/significance	Parameter;td.	dev.	z value	p value	Parameter;td.	dev.	z value	p value
constant	+2,52	+2,92	+0,86	+0,39	+1,97	+0,98	+2,00	+0,05**
position_EU	−0,22	+0,09	−2,42	+0,02**	−0,20	+0,07	−2,93	+0,00***
position_leftright	−0,01	+0,02	−0,72	+0,47				
position_extreme	+0,01	+0,05	+0,14	+0,89				
bailout state × leftright	+0,04	+0,03	+1,27	+0,20				
EFSF-1	−0,36	+1,99	−0,18	+0,86				
EFSF-2	+0,25	+0,77	+0,32	+0,75				
Fiscal Compact	+0,34	+0,48	+0,72	+0,47				
ESM	+0,42	+0,62	+0,68	+0,50				
bailout state	−0,97	+1,74	−0,56	+0,58				
fast-track parliament procedure	e +0,32	+0,58	+0,56	+0,58				
unemployment	−0,07	+0,13	−0,55	+0,58				
trust_national government	−0,09	+0,05	−1,76	+0,08*	−0,10	+0,05	−2,16	+0,03**
trust_national parliament	+0,13	+0,07	+1,96	+0,05**	+0,14	+0,06	+2,60	+0,01***
trust_EU	+0,03	+0,06	+0,42	+0,67				
effective_EU	−0,11	+0,10	−1,16	+0,25	−0,10	+0,05	−2,10	+0,04**
effective_national government	−0,00	+0,03	−0,17	+0,87				
McFadden's R²	0,48				0,46			
Corrected R²	0,31				0,41			
Akaike (AIC)	138,0				119,0			
Schwartz	189,3				134,1			

(Continued)

Table 4.2 (Continued)

Model type	Country variables							
Indep. variables	All				Selected			
Parameter/significance	Parameter;td.	dev.	z value	p value	parameter;td.	dev.	z value	p value
Hannan–Quinn	158,8				125,1			

$N = 151$; country-level clustered standard errors; variables selection based on test statistics
* significant at the 10% level
** significant at the 5% level
*** significant at the 1% level

Source: Author analysis

integration are reflected in the voting patterns of the European Parliament. However, if national parliamentary parties fail to 'normalize' EU policy-making, the European Parliament is also unlikely to achieve that goal. That is because most party groups reproduce the national lines of conflict (Borz and Rose, 2013). Furthermore, a failure to normalize policy-making within European economic governance is also likely to narrow the scope of valid arguments that could be employed in the discussion.

The findings of this chapter suggest a need to conduct further, longitudinal research on discourses accompanying political parties' voting behaviour. The question which remains to be answered is to what extent parties remain faithful to their positions once they move from the opposition to government and vice versa? Which factor is more important in predetermining parties' voting behaviour: their position regarding the European integration or membership in the government? Such analysis would help us to investigate in detail whether redistribution indeed lost relevance for national parties in decisions concerning European economic governance. Furthermore, the relation between national parties and European party groups requires further investigation. In particular, it has not been investigated yet to what extent European party groups indeed reproduce national lines of conflict concerning European economic governance.

Notes

1 Deputy Liam Twomey, 21 September 2011.
2 The states under study were: Austria, Belgium, Cyprus, Estonia, Finland, France, Germany, Greece, Ireland, Italy, Luxemburg, Malta, Netherlands, Portugal, Slovakia, Slovenia and Spain. Lithuania joined the euro only on 1 January 2015 and thus was not included in the analysis.
3 Courts have approved the extensive use of fast-track procedures.
4 http://www.efsf.europa.eu/about/index.htm
5 http://www.esm.europa.eu/
6 For Cyprus the data were not available.
7 There were two negative votes by government coalition parties: the DIMAR party in the combined vote on the ESM and the Fiscal Compact, and the Finnish Freedom Party against the Fiscal Compact.
8 The exceptions were Cyprus, where the data were not available, and Lithuania, which joined the eurozone only on 1 January 2015.
9 However, given the fact that the vast majority of MPs from the governing Syriza voted in favour of the third bailout programme and the conditionality accompanying it, we cannot exclude the possibility that radical left-wing parties, when in government, would prioritize 'responsibility' in their voting behaviour.

5 Parliamentary parties' discourses on anti-crisis measures
Between solidarity and particularistic interest[1]

Introduction

This chapter addresses the following questions: what were the major reasons that stood behind support or rejection of anti-crisis measures among national parliamentary parties? How convergent or divergent were parties in their choice of arguments supporting or rejecting anti-crisis measures? How can we explain the discursive differences among parliamentary parties?

It has been often observed that national parliaments are not only 'law-making' but also 'talking' institutional bodies. In particular, the major functions of national parliaments comprise not only of legislating and controlling governments but also of *legitimizing* outcomes of the legislative process. According to the literature (Blondel, 1973), national parliaments exercise three constitutive functions: law-making, representation of citizens and control of governments. Fulfilment of these functions depends to a large extent on communicative activity of national parliaments (Auel and Raunio, 2014a). In particular, communication remains central for the law-making process as it accounts for the quality and inclusiveness of deliberation. Representation of citizens would not be possible without communication: national parliaments rely on various channels and forms of communication in bringing national and European matters closer to their constituencies. Furthermore, the quality of the feedback that parliaments receive from their voters depends to a large extent on communicative practices. Finally, parliamentary control of governments' work also depends heavily on available forms of communication.

The link between voters and parliaments has been long recognized as crucial for the democratic legitimacy of decision-making processes at the EU level. Not surprisingly, scholarly attention towards communicative activities of national parliaments increased recently (Crespy and Schmidt, 2014). The initial focus remained on analyzing communicative practices between executives and parliaments; however, recent contributions have also focussed on analyzing how national parliaments communicate European matters to voters (Auel and Raunio, 2014a). The findings of the recent studies present a sobering picture: in general, the intensity and the quality of communication in European matters are not satisfactory. In particular, in plenary debates European matters are not intensively discussed; there has been also a lot of internal variation among particular parliaments (Auel and Raunio, 2014b). Plenary debates on European issues are more superficial in southern than northern European states (Lupato, 2014). Furthermore, national parliaments have not been particularly active employing new media in order to reach voters (Pollak and Slonimski, 2014). Against that background, national parliaments have not contributed particularly to closing the gap between the European Union level and national voters.

However, it has to be admitted that once a party or coalition obtains a majority after elections, approval of successive bills and policy measures does not depend on the discursive exchange of arguments. Nonetheless, parliamentarians need to justify their actions and decisions, and discourse constitutes an essential instrument for pursuing that goal (de Wilde, 2010; Wendler, 2011; Trenz and Michailidou, 2013). The arguments that parliamentarians use convey a justificatory logic, which, in turn, reveals their political preferences.

In order to legitimize or de-legitimize a given decision parliamentary parties employ political discourses. Parliamentarians have at their disposal various institutional forms of expressing their opinion publicly and engaging in argumentative exchange with other members of the parliament, such as, for instance, plenary debates, question hours or hearings. The arguments voiced publically by parliamentarians reach national public by means of mass-media. As a result, voters learn which arguments political parties employed in order to support or reject a given decision or a bill. Parliamentary parties are also aware that their arguments are to be evaluated by their constituencies.

This chapter analyzes in a qualitative and inductive manner which arguments parliamentary parties employed in order to support or reject the increased budgetary capacity of the European Financial Stability Facility (EFSF) as well as the Treaty on Stability, Coordination and Governance in the Economic and Monetary Union (Fiscal Compact) (see also: Closa and Maatsch, 2014). These two measures were selected for various reasons. First, while parliamentary debates on the EFSF revolve around solidarity among euro states, the discussion on the Fiscal Compact concentrated on new obligations in budgetary politics. As a consequence, focussing on these two measures allows investigating how parliamentary parties debate the two most important aspects of the European economic governance reform. Second, the debates on the EFSF and the Fiscal Compact are separated by the period of approximately two years' time (ratification of Fiscal Compact took place at different time in the euro states). As a result, it is also possible to observe whether particular parties changed their discourses. The empirical enquiry has been based on the analysis of plenary debates in lower chambers (unless there is a unicameral parliament in a given state) in the following states: Austria, Belgium, France, Germany, Greece, Ireland, Luxembourg, the Netherlands, Slovakia, Slovenia and Spain.

The study of parliamentary discourses can be perceived as supplementary to the analysis of vote outcomes presented in the prior chapter. In particular, discourses help us to establish *why* parliamentary parties supported or rejected a given bill. It can be well the case that support or opposition had various 'faces'. Hence, distinguishing between the reasons that motivate parties to vote in a particular way can also help us to establish which arguments drive – or hinder – consensus in European economic matters.

Analytical framework

The analysis presented in this chapter has been conducted in a semi-inductive manner. Namely, the exact content of arguments has not been anticipated but only the general categories, that is: pragmatic, ethical and moral (Habermas, 1991). *Pragmatic discourses* are those based on rationality oriented towards finalities. Once the finality is rationally established, the discourse presents the most efficient options for attaining these rational finalities. Actors pursuing consequential logic give reasons presenting a calculus of benefit and an optimal outcome in a given context. In pragmatic discourses conflict revolves around considerations of utility and/or efficiency.

In contrast, *ethical discourses* refer to the notion of 'good'. Ethical arguments put forward a specific community's view on constitutive values. Actions and decisions are recognized as legitimate when they comply with norms and conceptions which define the identity of a social group. Hence, conflict is likely to occur if different notions of 'good' are confronted with each other.

Finally, *moral arguments* aim at justifying political action by providing reasons that can be accepted as fair and just across different social groups with potentially conflicting interests or ethical values. In this sense, moral discourses convey arguments that, being accepted by all affected parties, can be universalized. Moral discourses systematically construct third parties or the 'other' as essential in their justification.

The relation to the 'other' makes it possible to distinguish between pragmatic, ethical and moral discourses. In pragmatic discourses, third parties are relevant only as a means to enable or restrict conditions for action. In ethical discourses, the 'other' is relevant only as far as he or she is interconnected with our own constellation of identity and interests. Hence, the other has only a relative importance. In moral discourses, taking the 'other' into account in conditions of equality is the central requirement for an acceptable outcome.

Methodological approach – frame analysis

Contemporary definitions of a 'frame' stress its interpretative notion (Tannen, 1993): in other words, frames are 'persistent patterns of cognition, interpretation and presentation of selection, emphasis and exclusion by which symbol-handlers routinely organize discourse' (Gitlin, 1980). Gamson and Modigliani (1989) define frames as interpretative packages at the core of which is a central organising idea, or frame, for making sense of relevant events, suggesting what is at issue. Frames also define problems, diagnose causes (Goffman, 1974 and 1981), make moral judgements and suggest remedies (de Vreese and Kandyla, 2009). In the course of the empirical analysis all frames that MPs used in their discourses were classified into the three categories of discourse: pragmatic, ethical and moral.

Frames, as speech acts, contain four major elements: (1) actors – the authors of statements (classified according to their political affiliation), (2) the subject of the statement (here, the parliamentary approval of the EFSF or the Fiscal Compact), (3) the direction of the statement (in favour or against) and (4) justifications (how the decision was framed). This analytical structure has been used in order to develop a 'code-book', an analytical tool enabling an empirical analysis in different states using the same procedure. The code-book was constructed in both a deductive and an inductive manner. Whereas categories 1, 2 and 3 were established prior to the empirical analysis, category 4 (frames) was further expanded during the analysis.

In the second step, when the coding process was finished, the data from all the countries were merged and analyzed in a comparative way, which helped to establish regular patterns in the discourses employed by parliamentary parties. The debates were analyzed (coded) in their original languages by the group of researchers who were proficient in these languages. The codes were assigned in English. The analysis has been conducted with help of the Atlas.ti software which allows systematic, qualitative analysis of discourses.

For instance, pragmatic frames reflected predominantly *interests*: in particular, MPs referred to *economic interests* of states, the eurozone or the European Union, and/or the *political interests* of specific euro states and institutions, such as governments or parliaments. MPs would also refer to the various *interests of banks*. The second group, ethical frames, included on the one hand, frames reflecting fears of diminishing national *sovereignty* in financial matters, and on the other, frames advocating *deeper political integration* of the EMU. The frame *responsibility for the euro and EU integration* stressed the fact that the euro currency is a project worthy of support. Hence, MPs who used that frame wished to demonstrate that the euro is an important component of the European integration project. MPs also referred to *breach* of EU legislation, in particular the Stability and Growth Pact and the no-bailout clause.

The third group, moral frames, consisted of frames referring to *solidarity and justice* and *social unjustness of austerity measures*. The former referred to solidarity among states or individuals in the name of universal justice. Regarding *austerity*, MPs would stress that the measure pushes common people, who are not responsible for generating the crisis, into deep poverty and hopelessness.

The empirical evidence has been based on plenary parliamentary debates accompanying the approval of the increased budgetary capacity of the EFSF and the Fiscal Compact in the following euro states: Austria, Belgium, France, Germany, Greece, Ireland, Luxembourg, the Netherlands, Slovakia, Slovenia and Spain.

Regarding the ratification process of the Fiscal Compact Ireland and Greece constituted special cases. In particular, in Ireland there was a referendum while in Greece the ratification of the Fiscal Compact was merged with the ratification of the ESM Treaty and the amendment of the Article 136(3) of the Lisbon Treaty. These specificities were also reflected in the content of plenary debates in these states.

Discursive support and opposition: dominant patterns

The empirical analysis of discourses demonstrated that there was little change in parliamentary parties' arguments throughout the analyzed time-period. As the previous chapter demonstrated, neither the voting patterns nor the discourses have changed over time. The major differences observed concerned country-specific peculiarities (e.g. the legislative merger in Greece). Furthermore, some ideas became more explicitly voiced. While already in 2010 parliamentary parties considered deepening integration in economic governance, two years later their ideas became more tangible.

According to the empirical findings, each of the two sub-groups of supporters and opponents employed specific discourses (see Table 5.1): pragmatic arguments revolving around national economic interests were the domain of governments (pragmatic supporters). Mainstream opposition parties, ergo idealistic supporters, referred predominantly to ethnical discourses pointing

Table 5.1 Dominant frames

Supporters	Political affiliation	Dominant frames
pragmatic	governing parties	economic interests (national and the European), responsibility for the eurozone
idealistic	mainstream opposition parties	economic interests, strengthening of EU integration in economic governance

Opponents	Political affiliation	Dominant frames
nationalistic	Eurosceptic, opposition, economic right	national economic interests, loss of sovereignty, breach of the SGP and the no-bailout rule
anti-austerians	Eurosceptic, opposition, economic left	solidarity (among states and people), social justice

Source: Adapted from Closa, C. and Maatsch, A. (2014) 'In a Spirit of Solidarity? Justifying the European Financial Stability Facility (EFSF) in National Parliamentary Debates', *Journal of Common Market Studies*, 52(4)

to the value of European integration process and the euro. Right-wing Eurosceptic opposition parties (nationalistic opponents) employed ethical arguments revolving around the fear of losing national sovereignty whereas left-wing Eurosceptic opposition parties (anti-austerians) employed moral discourses focussing on anti-solidaristic nature of anti-crisis measures.

The comparison of voting patterns and discourses reveals one asymmetry. In particular, some parliamentarians voted in favour of anti-crisis measures but, at the same time, they voiced critical statements. This asymmetry between voting and discourses has been also observed in other cases, for instance, parliamentary ratification of the Treaty of Lisbon (Maatsch, 2010). It is likely that these parliamentarians wanted to voice their criticism without endangering the completion of the ratification process. For instance, during the ratification of the Fiscal Compact parties which otherwise voted in favour of the Treaty pointed towards democratic deficit in the ratification procedure:

> *This is the first time any Government has brought a proposal for a European treaty to the Dáil without first publishing a White Paper. Past White Papers have served as a definitive statement of each treaty's implications in an Irish context. (. . .) This is a very bad start to a serious debate about a measure that is an important part of the wider agenda of restoring growth and job creation to Ireland and Europe. In effect the Government has ignored its duty under Standing Orders and*

precedent to provide Members of the Oireachtas with briefing sufficient to ensure a fully informed debate.

Many people are suffering today because of the impact of the recession. Unemployment is far too high and living standards are under pressure. However, we must remember the simple fact that both living standards and employment rates remain significantly higher than they would be if Ireland were outside the Union or the euro. (. . .) Let us not forget that the Union remains an immense force for good in areas such as equality, education and working conditions. People can summon up all of their ideological fury to condemn the Union as some elite conspiracy to do down ordinary people, but the reality is that it has done more for the people of Ireland and Europe than any left or right-wing ideology.[2]

Pragmatic and idealistic supporters

As already observed, the EFSF and the Fiscal Compact were discursively supported by governing parties and a share of opposition parties. The comparative analysis of discourses demonstrates that governing parties voiced different arguments than opposition parties. In particular, governing parties were more likely to refer to pragmatic arguments, such as economic interests of their states:

I am voting "Yes" because I believe it helps us. My point today is that voting "No" genuinely will not help Ireland's recovery, it will hinder it. If the stability treaty is about anything, it is about making sure grave mistakes are not made again. It is about getting a sustainable, fair and people-focused economy here in Ireland and across Europe, where public money is available for public services and job incentives, not for paying down debt. In addition, as I have said on many occasions, it is about the euro in our pocket.[3]

The analysis demonstrates very clearly that governing parties[4] supported both anti-crisis measures because they were convinced that the measures served their domestic interests. By the same token, these parties demonstrated a very pragmatic, output-oriented approach towards the reform of European economic governance based on a very 'functional' logic of justification according to which a 'problem' needed to be addressed (or avoided) and ethical and/or moral considerations were deemed to be less important. Governing parties would rarely refer to solidarity despite the fact that the legal basis for the mechanism refers to the principle of solidarity. They rather avoided statements which could suggest that European economic governance became more Europeanized or that the current reform opened up a possibility of further integration. Instead, they would point towards a potential spillover of the crisis to other states. Hence, governing parties spoke primarily of economic interests of their own countries and the eurozone:

> *Ladies and Gentlemen! Who believes that, what we are doing here today, namely the extension of the bailout fund, is done in order to save Greece, is wrong. (call from the MP Bucher: In order to save banks! The German and the French banks!) We do it in order to stabilize the eurozone, my Ladies and Gentlemen – euro is **our** currency, these are **our** salaries and pensions, **our** savings. – We are acting very egoistically here: it concerns **our** money, my Ladies and Gentlemen, and not a rescue of Greece.*[5]

Governing parties also referred to political responsibility for the eurozone. They would present euro as a common good of its citizens which not only safeguards their economic prosperity but also unites them. In these respects, governing parties also voiced ethical arguments referring to common values of the European Union:

> *In this spirit I tell you: what we ratify here today is a very important step to demonstrate to the World that we stand for Euro. We want it as our stable currency. We believe that we can manage better our economic activity with it and that we can prosper better with it. For these reasons I ask you all here for your support.*[6]

The group of 'idealistic' supporters was composed of mainstream opposition parties.[7] Opposition parties, contrary to governing parties, justified their support predominantly with ethical arguments pointing towards political values of the European Union and the value of European integration process as such. Interestingly, mainstream opposition parties perceived the reform of European economic governance as a possible prelude to the fiscal union:

> *In fact, it is necessary to proceed towards a real economic governance of the euro zone which, as we know, will take years to implement. That's what the centrists have always demanded: a real European federalism.*[8]

Apart from that, mainstream opposition parties also frequently raised pragmatic, economic arguments referring to national economic interests or economic interests of the eurozone as a whole.

Opponents: nationalists and anti-austerians

In the course of the analysis it was possible to identify two sub-groups of opponents. Both groups were composed of parties recognized as Eurosceptic,[9] however, the 'nationalist' group was composed of economically right-wing parties[10] while the 'anti-austerians' was composed of left-wing Eurosceptic parties.[11] In sum, Eurosceptic parties contested anti-crisis measures both in their voting behaviour and in their discourses.

'Nationalist' opponents, mostly found in Austria, Belgium, the Netherlands, Slovakia and Slovenia, were driven predominantly by national economic interests. They claimed to represent the interests of national taxpayers who are assumed to share the burden of crisis although they had not contributed to it in any manner.

> *It cannot be the case that you take away from the sovereign the right to decide about her founds, namely tax payers' money, so that the Austrian sovereign is forced to pump her tax payers' money into shabby banking systems and bankrupt states for which she does not hold any responsibility.*[12]
>
> *My highly honoured Ladies and Gentlemen, you should face it: today you decide to take up 29 billion euro liability – SPÖ, ÖVP and the Greens all together. 29 billion! That is almost a half of our national budget! 29 billion from taxes – the money we do not have, the money that we in Austria do not generate (MP Ing. Westenhaler: it's a crime!), the money that we have to take from credits, my dear Ladies and Gentlemen. (. . .). 29 billion euro – the money we will never see again, the money of the Austrian taxpayers which will not bring any profits to the Austrian citizens. That is the reality, my dear Ladies and Gentlemen!*[13]

These opponents justified their opposition towards the EFSF and the Fiscal Compact with national economic interests, fear of losing national sovereignty over financial policy and breach of the Stability and Growth Pact (SGP). In particular, they attributed the responsibility for the crisis to southern European governments' politics. As a consequence, the nationalist opponents argued that had the SGP been respected, the financial crisis could have been avoided. In the opinion of 'nationalist' opponents, the EFSF constituted the breach of the no-bailout clause. Therefore, in their discourses they presented themselves as guardians of the EU treaties. Finally, both the EFSF and the Fiscal Compact were said to violate national sovereignty in fiscal matters.

While the prior group of opponents referred predominantly to particularistic, national interests, the second group, 'anti-austerians', brought moral arguments to the discussion. Anti-austerians, mostly found in Germany and

Greece, focussed predominantly on austerity. As a consequence, they justified their negative stance on the EFSF and the Fiscal Compact with moral arguments such as the lack of solidarity with common people suffering under austerity measures. Anti-austerians argued that banks are responsible for the crisis; however, the decision-makers shifted the responsibility for the crisis from banks to individual taxpayers. In their opinion, it has been immoral to cut spending on social care or increase taxes for the poorest while bank directors have not been held responsible for their actions.

Today I have rejected the so called bailout, because I am against politics which is unconditionally subordinated to profits of banks and enterprises. Today I have said no to politics which does not represent interests of the majority of the population but rather interests of banks, speculators and financial elites. (Hans-Michael Goldmann (FDP): What nonsense!) You are solidaristic with gangs of gamblers, the financial mafia. We are solidaristic with people who have to experience the crisis because of the German economic policy which led to wage dumping over the last few years. We are solidaristic with people in Greece who protest against your slush-programs and bailouts. We are solidaristic with people in Portugal and Ireland who say no to Europe which is unsocial and unjust. For these reasons I have voted against today.[14]

In contrast to the mainstream governing and opposition parties, anti-austerians raised very sceptical opinions regarding the efficiency of austerity measures. They rejected the EFSF and the Fiscal Compact arguing that these two measures promote austerity. Instead, anti-austerians advocated introduction of interventionist policies aiming at promoting growth and employment:

Austerity and growth do not go hand in hand. The Tánaiste is wrong to claim one can pursue an aggressive strategy of cutbacks and other austerity measures and expect economic growth. If he examines the recent past, he will see evidence that austerity damages prospects for growth and has a deep and damaging effect on the domestic economy. Sinn Féin believes the treaty, as with much of the policy that preceded it, is bad for Ireland and the European Union.[15]

Anti-austerians also pointed frequently towards the democratic deficit of the reform process. For instance, they observed that the most important decisions have taken place at the intergovernmental level and that national parliaments were not properly consulted:

Tell them [the German voters] that in the future they will elect a Parliament that will not have much to say because Germany belongs to states which debt-level exceeds what the Fiscal Pact requires. Tell the people that this is a coup d'état against the constitution.[16]

Solidarity, understood as a European principle, played a very interesting role in anti-austerians' discourses. Namely, in contrast to mainstream opposition parties, anti-austerians argued that the EFSF does not foster solidarity among European states but rather violates it. In their opinion the bailout fund promotes conditionality, not solidarity. As anti-austerians noted, the suffering of common people affected by austerity measures cannot be reconciled with the modern understanding of social justice.

Plenary debates devoted to ratification of the Fiscal Compact in Greece revealed an additional, country-specific discourse. This is because Fiscal Compact had been ratified as a legislative package (merger). The bill, which has been submitted by the Standing Committee of Economic Issues for debate in the plenary, was composed of 5 Articles: Article 1 on ratification of the Decision of the European Council that amends Article 136 of the Treaty on the Functioning of the EU; Article 2 on ratification of the Treaty establishing the European Stability Mechanism; Article 3 on ratification of the Treaty on Stability, Coordination and Governance in the Economic and Monetary Union; Article 4 stipulating additional amendments related to the banking system, the creation of a special account in the Bank of Greece for priority public-debt service (financed by the EFSF and the Greek state) as well as Article 5 stipulating the terms of this bill's entry into law. The extraordinary procedure was perceived as highly controversial by many parliamentarians. In fact, the procedure itself, or the question of its constitutionality, received as much parliamentary attention as the discussion on the content of the bill. Furthermore, lack of constitutionality of the bill was also employed as an argument against the ratification of the Fiscal Compact.

The governing PASOK and the ND defended the special procedure arguing that the bill does not envisage changes in institutional competences (delegation of power) or giving up of national sovereignty. Therefore, it would not be necessary to ratify it with a special majority. The opponents, such as LAOS, SYRIZA or KKE, argued that the discussion on procedural issues should have preceded the debate on the content of the bill. However, in practice, Greek parliamentarians had been forced to discuss the procedure and the content of the bill during one plenary session. The opponents of the procedure also observed that constitutional change should not be approved through a special procedure. Furthermore, in their view, the procedure disempowered the national parliament in Greece because it limited the time envisaged for discussion. The communist KKE has even observed that the special procedure is not democratic and that it serves interests of the bourgeois.

Conclusions

The comparative analysis of plenary parliamentary discourses presented in this chapter proved to play a very important role in reconstructing retrospectively national conflict lines accompanying the reform of European economic governance. The knowledge acquired through the analysis of discourses has a particular added value for it not only complements the comparative study of voting patterns but it also helps us to grasp the variety of reasons that have stood behind support or opposition towards particular anti-crisis measures.

On the general level, the analysis demonstrated that some parties tended to be more critical in their discourses than in their voting behaviour. Plenary debates constituted an opportunity for parliamentary parties to raise their concerns and criticism without endangering the outcome of the ratification process. An in-depth analysis of plenary discourses demonstrated that neither support nor the opposition was a unitary discursive construct. In particular, while supporters were divided into pragmatic and idealistic ones, the group of opponents comprised two distinct sub-groups: nationalists and anti-austerians. Each of the four sub-groups prioritized different discourses: pragmatic supporters prioritized pragmatic discourses and idealistic supporters – ethnical ones. In comparison, nationalistic supporters referred predominantly to pragmatic arguments whilst the anti-austerians to moral ones.

Pragmatic supporters, composed of governing parties, referred predominantly to particularistic national economic interests. In contrast, idealistic supporters, represented by mainstream opposition parties, employed more frequently ethical arguments referring to political value of the European Union and the value of the European integration process as such. Referring predominantly to national interests, governing parties appealed to the lowest common denominator which could mobilize hesitant parliamentarians to ratify anti-crisis measures. As a consequence, governing parties have not mentioned the possibility of deepening the integration process probably in order not to discourage more conservative or slightly Eurosceptic parties. Justifying support for the EFSF or the Fiscal Compact with national economic interests very likely appeared to be the most reasonable support-winning strategy, particularly among hesitant and slightly Eurosceptic parliamentarians. In sum, the major drivers of the institutional reform were pragmatic and ethical discourses. Although the reforms, and particularly the establishment of the bailout fund, implied a basic solidarity among member states, supporters of the reforms decided not to employ moral arguments (see also Closa and Maatsch, 2014). Rather, it was far more common among the supporters to refer to 'the spirit of positive conditionality' inspiring the institutional reform in general.

The discursive opponents of the analyzed anti-crisis measures employed two very different types of discourses. Both groups were composed of Eurosceptic parties; however, the nationalists were represented by the right-wing Europsceptic parties whereas anti-austerians by the left-wing Eurosceptic parties. Nationalists rejected the analyzed anti-crisis measures pointing predominantly to national economic or political interests. They would also justify their position with treaty articles forbidding bailout. In their narrative the responsibility for the crisis has been attributed to southern European states. In contrast, anti-austerians rejected the analyzed measures due to solidarity with citizens of southern European states. These parties argued that decision-makers burdened common people with the costs of the crisis whereas individual and institutional actors responsible for triggering the crisis have not been held responsible. According to anti-austerians, austerity measures are economically harmful as they do not help to generate growth or combat unemployment. Furthermore, austerity cannot be reconciled with the basic social justice as these policies systematically disadvantage the most vulnerable social groups. Therefore, whereas discourses of nationalist opponents manifested their disagreement towards deepening of European integration in economic matters, anti-austerians disapproved of the rules (conditionality) and forms (fast-track measures) of implementation, but not the very idea of establishing a bailout fund or reforming the Stability and Growth Pact. As a consequence, the political consequences of nationalists' and anti-austerians' opposition are very different.

Interestingly, these were Eurosceptic anti-austerians which most frequently raised the issue of national parliaments' disempowerment in the reform process of European economic governance. Mainstream parties, the governing and the opposition ones, have hardly tackled the issue. Throughout the ratification process of anti-crisis measures parliamentarians discussed strengthening of the integration process in European economic governance. Particularly the debates accompanying the ratification of the Fiscal Compact demonstrated that parties mean very different things when they discuss deepening of economic integration. In particular, while for some parties the idea implied stronger intergovernmental control in that policy area, there were parties which advocated political or fiscal union with a European ministry of finance.

In sum, it can be observed that parliamentary parties, despite their limited oversight and decision-making powers in the reform process of European economic governance, remained well-informed about the particularities of each debated institutional measure. At this place it should be reminded that parliamentary parties worked under considerable time pressure. Furthermore, not all parties were thoroughly briefed by their governments (i.e. via question hours), hence, there many parties that suffered under significant information-deficit. Finally, it has to be observed that the vast majority of parliamentary parties established and articulated very clearly their positions. That finding demonstrates that parliamentary parties 'have done their homework' consisting, in this case, of processing a huge amount of new information and developing an official stance in congruence with their ideological stances.

Notes

1 This chapter of the book draws, to a limited extent, on the article presenting preliminary results of the analysis that initially covered only the approval of the increased capacity of the EFSF. In contrast to this book chapter, the pilot study employed a more quantitative approach. In order to compare both studies, see: Closa, C. and Maatsch, A. (2014) 'In a Spirit of Solidarity? Justifying the European Financial Stability Facility (EFSF) in National Parliamentary Debates'. *Journal of Common Market Studies*, 52(4), 826–842.
2 Seán Ó Fearghaíl, Fianna Fíil, Dáil Èreann, 18.04.2012.
3 Eamon Gilmore, Labour, Dáil Èreann, 18.04.2012.
4 Examples of government parties (at the moment of the analysis) which employed pragmatic discourses: Austria (SPÖ, ÖVP), Belgium (CD&V, MR, spa, CDH, Open VLD, PS), France (UMP, PS, NC), Germany (CDU/CSU, FDP), Greece (PASOK, ND), Ireland (Labour, Fine Gael), Luxembourg (CSV, LSAP), the Netherlands (VVD, CDA, PVV, PvdA), Slovakia (SDKU'-DS, SMER-SD), Slovenia (SDS, LDS, Zares, DESUS, DL, SLS), Spain (PSOE, PP). The exhaustive list of parties and their political affiliation is provided in Chapter 4.
5 'Meine Damen und Herren! Wer da noch glaubt, dass wir das, was wir heute tun, näm-lich die Erweiterung des Haftungsschirms beschließen, tun, um Griechenland zu retten, der irrt. (Abg. Bucher: Um die Banken zu retten! Die deutschen und französischen Banken!) Das tun wir, um die Stabilität des Euro zu sichern, meine Damen und Herren – und der Euro ist unser Geld, das sind unsere Löhne und Gehälter, unsere Pensionen, unsere Sparguthaben. – Wir handeln hier sehr egoistisch: Wir handeln für unser Geld, meine Damen und Herren, und nicht zur Rettung Griechenlands.' Austria, Nationalrat, Dr. Günter Stummvoll (ÖVP), 30.09.2011
6 'In diesem Sinne sage ich: Was wir heute beschließen, ist ein wichtiger Schritt, um der Welt deutlich zu machen: Wir stehen zum Euro. Wir wollen ihn als unsere stabile Währung. Wir glauben, dass wir mit ihm besser wirtschaften können, besser in Wohlstand leben können. Deshalb werbe ich um Ihrer aller Zustimmung,' the German Chancellor Dr. Angela Merkel, Bundestag, 29.06.2012.
7 Examples of parliamentary opposition parties (at the moment of the analysis) which employed ethical discourses supporting anti-crisis measures: Austria (Greens), Belgium (PS, MR), France (UMP, PS), Germany (SPD, Greens), Greece (ND, DISY), Ireland (Labour, Fianna Fáil), Luxembourg (déi Greng, DP), the Netherlands (D66, GL) Slovakia (KDH, SDKU-DS), Slovenia (SD), Spain (PP, PSOE). The exhaustive list of parties and their affiliations is provided in Chapter 4.
8 'Enfin, il faut aller vers une vraie gouvernance économique de la zone euro, et celle-ci, nous le savons bien, mettra des années à se mettre en place. C'est ce que les centristes ont toujours demandé : un véritable fédéralisme européen.' France, Assemblée nationale, Charles de Courson (Nouveau Centre), 06.09.2011.

9 According to the PIREDEU database.
10 Examples of right-wing Eurosceptic parties which opposed the analyzed anti-crisis measures due to ethical arguments revolving around national sovereignty: Austria (FPÖ), Belgium (LDD, VB), Greece (LAOS), Luxembourg (ADR), the Netherlands (PVV), Slovakia (SaS). For detailed information see Chapter 4.
11 Examples of left-wing Eurosceptic parties which rejected the analyzed anti-crisis measures due to austerity: France (GDR), Germany (The Left), Greece (Syriza), Ireland (Sinn Féin). For detailed information see Chapter 4.
12 'Es kann nicht sein, dass Sie dem Souverän sein Recht nehmen wollen, über seine Gelder, nämlich Steuergelder, verfügen zu wollen, sodass der österreichische Souverän durch Sie heute – durch diese drei Parteien – gezwungen werden soll, sein Steuergeld in **marode Bankensysteme** und **Pleitestaaten** zu pumpen, für die er keine Verantwortung trägt.' 4–5.07. 2012, Nationalrat, Heinz-Christian Strache (FPÖ).
13 'Meine sehr geehrten Damen und Herren, das sollten Sie einmal auf der Zunge zergehen lassen: 29 Milliarden € Zahlungsverpflichtungen beschließen Sie heute – SPÖ, ÖVP und Grüne gemeinsam. 29 Milliarden €! Das ist fast die Hälfte unseres österreichischen Staatshaushaltes! 29 Milliarden € an Steuergeld – Geld, das wir nicht haben, Geld, das wir in Österreich nicht erwirtschaften (Abg. Ing. Westenthaler: Ein Verbrechen!), Geld, das wir in Form von Krediten aufnehmen müssen, meine sehr geehrten Damen und Herren. (. . . .) 29 Milliarden € – Geld, das wir nie mehr wiedersehen, Geld, von dem die österreichischen Steuerzahler, die Bürger in Österreich keinen Nutzen haben. Das ist die Realität, meine sehr geehrten Damen und Herren!' Austria, Nationalrat, Josef Bucher (BZÖ), 30.09.2011
14 'Ich habe heute diesen sogenannten Rettungsschirm abgelehnt, weil ich eine Politik ablehne, die sich den Profitwünschen der Banken und Konzerne bedingungsos unterordnet. Ich sagte heute Nein zu einer Politik, die nicht den Interessen der Mehrheit der Bevölkerung, son-dern vor allem denen der Banken, Spekulanten und oberen Zehntausend dient.(Hans-Michael Goldmann [FDP]: Was für ein Unsinn!) Ihre Solidarität gilt nur diesen Zockerbanden, der Finanzmafia. Unsere Solidarität gilt stattdessen den Menschen in den Ländern, die diese Krise aufgrund der von Ihnen betriebenen deutschen Wirtschaftspolitik, die in den letzten Jahren zu Lohndumping führte, durchleben müssen. Unsere Solidarität gilt den Menschen, die sich in Griechenland gegen die Kürzungsprogramme und die Rettungsringe aus Blei, die Sie ihnen vorwerfen, erheben. Wir sind solidarisch mit den Menschen in Portugal und Irland, die Nein sagen zu einem Europa, das unsozial und ungerecht ist. Deshalb habe ich heute mit Nein gestimmt.' Germany, Bundestag, Sevim Dağdelen (DIE LINKE): 29.09.2011.
15 Mary Lou McDonand, Sinn Féin, 18.04.2012 Dáil Éireann.
16 'Sagen Sie ihnen, dass sie in Zukunft auch in Deutschland ein Parlament wählen dürfen, das nicht mehr viel zu sagen haben wird; denn auch Deutschland gehört zu den Ländern, deren Staatsverschuldung weit über dem liegt, was der Fiskalpakt verlangt. Sagen Sie den Menschen, dass das ein kalter Putsch gegen das Grundgesetz ist.' Sahra Wagenknecht, Bundestag, 29.06.2012.

6 Macroeconomic preferences of national parliamentary parties[1]

Introduction

The fourth and the fifth chapter of this book analyzed how parliamentary parties voted on anti-crisis measures and why they supported or rejected them. The analysis of voting behaviour established that the dominant explanatory variable has been political parties' position on European integration. In particular, whereas pro-European parties voted in favour of anti-crisis measures, Eurosceptic parties rejected them. The comparative analysis of discourses accompanying approval of the analyzed measures demonstrated that parties supporting the measures referred to general economic interests of their states and the eurozone as well as the value of the European integration process in general. Opponents tended to justify their position with national interests and narrow interpretation of the 'no bailout clause' but also negative effects of austerity measures on the bailout states' economies. It is telling that the legislative process concerning macroeconomic reform has been to such extent devoid of arguments discussing different models of markets' stabilization. Apparently, only a small share of opponents raised the issue debating the neoliberal approach.

In fact, the reform of European economic governance is not only a matter of 'more or less' integration (Jabko, 2011), but it is also about redistribution and a choice of economic strategies oriented towards combating the crisis. Furthermore, voters can be adequately represented only if parties demonstrate how a particular policy or legislative bills affects their interests. Do these findings imply that the majority of parliamentary parties do not have an opinion on that matter? Is it likely that parties representing different positions on the left–right scale have not advocated different policy options? This chapter analyzes the issue in more detail.

The chapter poses the following questions: do economic principles inform political parties' choices regarding anti-crisis measures in the eurozone or, on the contrary, is it the newly emerged conflict of interest between the creditors and debtors? The literature suggests that macroeconomic policy outcomes, both during economic booms and downturns, depend to a large extent on the economic stance of the governing party: whereas parties representing the economic left advocate Keynesian macroeconomic measures, right-wing parties opt for neoliberal ones (Alesina and Rosenthal, 1995; Boix, 2000). However, the existing literature referred to policies that political parties were propagating for their own country and not for other states. As a consequence, we do not know whether the same mechanism accounts for the choice of anti-crisis policies which political parties advocate for the bailout states in the eurozone. Prior policy-responses to financial crises were always national ones (though with some degree of international coordination, for instance, under the International Monetary Fund), but the financial crisis that hit the eurozone in 2010 urged not only a joint coordination of national policies but, foremost, financial solidarity among the eurozone members (Closa and Maatsch, 2014).

The current political discourse challenges the established knowledge regarding the role of economic principles in political parties' policy choices. The creditors are blamed of pursuing the 'hellenization' of the crisis (Krugman, 2012) by claiming that financial problems of southern Europe are predominantly caused by their governments' irresponsible budgetary policy. On the other hand, governments of debtors reject that interpretation and point to systemic weaknesses of the euro as a common currency. Whereas societies in creditor states remain reluctant towards financial assistance, taxpayers in debtor states demonstrate their frustration with harsh austerity measures.

By now, the literature has neglected the role of parliamentary deliberation on anti-crisis measures. Political scientists devoted more attention to decision-making processes at the executive level (Puetter, 2012) than among legislators. However, these are parliamentary debates which account most directly for policy-formation processes on a domestic level. In contrast to executives, parliamentary discourses represent more thoroughly a diversity of interests and positions expressed by political actors (Wendler, 2013).

This chapter poses the following specific research questions: how can we explain parliamentary parties' positioning on anti-crisis measures implemented in the bailout states of the eurozone? Which factors account for political parties' choices: the economic orientation of a party, conflicting interests of creditors and debtors or perhaps the cleavage between the government and the opposition?[2] The empirical findings draw on national plenary parliamentary debates devoted to the approval of the increased budgetary capacity of the European Financial Stability Facility (EFSF) from 2011. The selected states were: Austria, Germany, France, Slovenia, Belgium, Spain, Ireland and Greece.

The methodological approach of the chapter was based, first, on the qualitative and quantitative discourse analysis of national parliamentary debates devoted to the increased budgetary capacity of the EFSF and, second, on the QCA crisp-set analysis. Whereas plenary discourses helped to establish which parties supported neoliberal and Keynesian measures, the QCA analysis was employed in order to examine the conditions under which parties opted for one of the two macroeconomic approaches.

The chapter begins with a presentation of two macroeconomic approaches: Keynesianism and neoliberalism. The next section of the chapter presents the literature review and the hypotheses accounting for political parties' positioning on macroeconomic policies. The empirical analysis section is preceded by the presentation of the methodological approach. The final section of the chapter presents conclusions.

Keynesianism and neoliberalism

Both approaches differ significantly with respect to the role a state should play in the market cycle. In general, neoliberals stress deregulation, whereas Keynesians advocate an active role of a state in monetary and fiscal policy. Although both neoliberals and Keynesians share the assumption that markets act rationally, neoliberals argue that markets always get the price right provided all the relevant information is publically available. Keynesians, by contrast, point to various 'market failures' which distort the situation of a perfect competition.

How should governments respond to the economic crisis? Keynesians and neoliberals recommend the opposite: neoliberal economists advocate pro-cyclical measures and Keynesians counter-cyclical ones. According to Keynesians, governments should stimulate the economy by conducting expansionary fiscal and monetary policy, that is, increasing government spending, increasing inflation and decreasing the tax rate. In contrast, neoliberal economists argue that government spending is counterproductive during recessions for it tends to lead to stagflation (inflation and unemployment increase while growth decreases). Instead, neoliberals suggest budgetary consolidation, policies of austerity which aim at reducing public expenses.

The neoliberal tool-box for states struggling with economic crisis comprises predominantly budgetary consolidation and various austerity measures. Economists representing this approach maintain that strong austerity not only allows a reduction in public spending but, foremost, it helps to regain confidence in the markets (Ardagna, 2009). From that perspective, markets are believed to lose confidence in states that continue to run high deficits. These states are likely to be 'punished' by investors with higher interest rates. Neoliberal economists disregard Keynesian anti-crisis measures by arguing that the only viable strategy to lead the economy out of the crisis and to regain confidence of investors is to cut public spending in order to reduce the deficit. In their view, expansionary fiscal policy will increase interest rates and thereby reduce investment and consumption.

Keynesian economists are not against budgetary consolidation as such, but they argue that it should be implemented during periods of economic growth and not vice versa. In their view, strong austerity leads to decrease of the GDP (Guajardo et al., 2011). Although the reduction of spending allows governments to cut the deficit, the GDP is very likely to a decrease because cuts in public spending (including reductions of work-places in public sector) are likely to weaken consumption. That, in turn, affects the private sector which is going to sell less. Therefore, Keynesians believe that inflation is a better tool to 'get the prices right' than wage-cuts suggested by neoliberals. Under higher inflation investors may be more willing to borrow if the currency is going to be worth less.

Contrary to neoliberals, Keynesians point to the fact that prices and wages can only slowly adjust to the economic downturn. As Mankiw and Romer (1991) observed, prices adjust slowly (they are 'sticky') due to 'menu costs' which are related to the adaptation process, such as printing new menu lists in restaurants.

Despite a large body of literature in that area, there is no consensus among empirically oriented economists as to which of the two approaches is more effective during the crisis (Furceri and Sousa, 2009). Some studies indicate that governments' spending has a negative effect on consumption and investment. Others stipulate that high sovereign debt levels (the effect of public spending) hamper growth (Kumar and Woo, 2011; Cottarelli and Jaramillo, 2012). By contrast, there are also empirical studies which conclude that public spending offers a better way out of crisis by having a positive effect on investment and consumption (Furceri and Sousa, 2009; Baldacci, Gupta and Mulas-Granados, 2012).

Which factors account for political parties' positioning on macroeconomic policies? Hypotheses of this study

The existing literature identified major factors explaining political parties' positioning on macroeconomic policies, such as general economic ideology (left or right) or governing status (membership in the government or opposition). However, the question remains: do the same explanatory paths account for political parties' choices on macroeconomic measures during the current sovereign debt crisis? The QCA is an adequate approach to test that because it allows investigating 'conjunctual causations' across the observed cases. In other words, we assume that different constellations of factors may lead to the same result (i.e. Keynesian positioning). Furthermore, each constellation leading to the same outcome can have a different theoretical significance: whereas one can imply that 'crisis matters', the other can demonstrate the opposite. This section sheds more light on phenomenon.

The existing empirical research demonstrated that *parliamentary parties opt for macroeconomic measures which coincide with their general economic ideology: parties located on the economic 'right' opt for neoliberal measures whereas parties located on the economic 'left' – advocate Keynesian ones* (Alesina and Rosenthal, 1995; Boix, 2000). For instance, in the United States the Republicans concentrate on decreasing inflation, but the Democrats attach more importance to the reduction of unemployment. More recent literature focussing on the financial crisis (i.e. Broz, 2013) also demonstrates that economic orientation of governments plays a significant role. According to Broz (2013) partisan character of governments can be a cause of a financial crisis. This is because right-wing governments introduce various deregulative measures. Therefore, a response – like the run-up – to a crisis is also likely to be informed by the economic ideology of a governing political party. In particular, political parties representing the right-wing of the economic spectrum are likely to advocate pro-cyclical measures, such as policies of austerity. In contrast, parties representing the economic left are more likely to propose anti-cyclical measures, for instance, increase of government spending.

According to the other hypothesis put forward in the literature institutional factors are likely to modify MPs' macroeconomic positions. In particular, given the fact that the major cleavage in politics is between governments and opposition (e.g. Raunio, 2009), we can assume governing parties to continue the once implemented policy line, whereas opposition parties continue to challenge it and propose alternative solutions. Furthermore, whereas governing majorities carry the burden of international responsibility for their position, opposition parties are free from those considerations.

In the eurozone context the cleavage between the government and the opposition can also account for the choice of macroeconomic measures. There were two major reasons why parties in government became wedded to neoliberal macroeconomic policies at the EU level. First, already before the sovereign debt crisis the EMU and the SGP were based on neoliberal principles. Second, having opted for a neoliberal anti-crisis approach in 2010, governing parties decided to continue with that policy line in 2011 despite opposition parties' criticism. On the contrary, opposition parties are more likely to support Keynesian measures. They enjoy an advantaged position since they are not obliged to implement the policies they are suggesting. Moreover, opposition parties can attract new voters who are dissatisfied with the current policy line. As a consequence, we can assume that *whereas governing parties are more likely to continue with the neoliberal policies, opposition parties are expected to propose counter-measures (Keynesian ones)*.

However, we have to bear in mind that the abovementioned mechanisms were established upon the data analyzing macroeconomic policies which national parties implemented in their own states. Until now, there is no research demonstrating how the creditor or debtor statuses can interfere with the abovementioned mechanisms. There are certain reasons which allow us to expect that the sovereign debt crisis in the eurozone generated new paths accounting for the choice of macroeconomic measures. Namely, there is one, but very important, difference between the current crisis of the eurozone and all other prior crises: eurozone states are affected by the crisis even if their finances are healthy. Obviously, in the globalized economy financial crisis in one state affects other states as well, for instance, by impacting the import–export rates. However, the interdependence of national economies in the eurozone is even stronger. This is because creditor states carry the risk of covering debtor states' debts if they fail to attend it. Furthermore, in contrast to the IMF, these are only eurozone members that can apply for a loan.

The second peculiarity of the eurozone crisis is that creditors decide on anti-crisis measures that do not apply to their own states but to the bailout states. Although in principle national finances remain within the exclusive competences of national governments, debtors have to give up some sovereignty once they sign the Memorandum of Understanding (MoE). Acquisition of loans from the IMF also involves conditionality; however, their mechanism is less politicized than in the eurozone. In the eurozone these were national governments and national parliaments that had to approve the introduction of the bailout fund. By definition, these institutions follow their national political and economic interests. Under unanimity procedure, a veto of one eurozone member can put on hold the approval process of the bailout fund. That situation can give rise to conflicting interests of creditors and debtors but also frustration among constituencies in both groups of states.

Hence, if the sovereign debt crisis had an impact on political parties' macroeconomic choices it can be expected that *parliamentary parties in states that received a bailout are more inclined to opt for Keynesian anti-crisis measures. Vice versa, states with stable economies would be more likely to opt for neoliberal anti-crisis measures.*

Why do Keynesian anti-crisis measures better correspond with the interests of 'weak' economies? That is because voters in these states strongly disapprove of austerity measures. For that reason, as a vote-seeking strategy, it is risky for MPs to advocate introduction of such measures in their states. In contrast, Keynesian anti-crisis measures are more likely to be welcomed by voters. If governments 'inject' money into the market their voters will not punish them in the next elections.

On the other hand, it can be expected that stable economies, unlikely to need a bailout themselves, would be more reluctant towards Keynesian anti-crisis measures. Why? Weak economies in the eurozone cannot increase their public deficit without risking a further increase of interest rates, particularly if they already have liquidity problems (southern Europe) or solvency problems (Greece). As some economists observed (de Grauwe and Ji, 2012), financial markets underpriced risk of southern European states before the crisis and overpriced it during the crisis, which was not the case of states with national currencies. Governments of states in the monetary union are more prone to 'self-fulfilling liquidity problem' (de Grauwe and Ji, 2012, p. 887) than states with national currencies. That is because markets are more afraid of default in the case of shared currency. Hence, if eurozone states opted for Keynesian anti-crisis measures (for instance, a fiscal stimulus), financial markets would very likely respond by increasing further the interest rates. As a consequence, in order to avoid panic of financial markets, such a fiscal stimulus would have to be financed (or at least co-financed) externally, that is either from the EU budget or by economically stable euro states.

On that background this chapter puts forward two sets of hypotheses. The first one reflects the 'state of the art' in the literature where the impact of the eurozone sovereign debt crisis on parties' positioning has not been envisaged yet. If the sovereign debt crisis did not influence parties' positioning on macroeconomic measures, we can assume that the conditions accounting for Keynesian positioning are: left-wing orientation of a party and membership in the opposition, ~R*~gov→K (see Table 6.1 for the explanation of symbols). On the other hand, the conditions accounting for neoliberal

Table 6.1 Explanation of codes used in the QCA model

Conditions and the outcome	Symbols	Value	Explanation
Outcome	K	1	Keynesian positioning
Outcome	~K	0	Neoliberal positioning
Condition	R	1	Economic right
Condition	~R	0	Economic left
Condition	gov	1	Government affiliation
Condition	~gov	0	Opposition affiliation
Condition	bailout	1	Prior bailout
Condition	~bailout	0	No bailout received

Source: Author

positioning are: right-wing orientation and membership in the government, R*gov→~K.

If the sovereign debt crisis *did* have an impact on positioning of political parties, the two paths accounting for Keynesian positioning are: (I-a) bailout→K or (II-a) bailout* R*gov→K. Correspondingly, the paths accounting for neoliberal positioning are: (I-b) ~bailout→~K or (II-b) ~bailout*~R*gov→K. The paths (I-a) and (I-b) simply acknowledge the impact of the bailout (its presence and absence) on parties' positioning. On the other hand, the paths (II-a) and (II-b) constitute hard cases from the perspective of the state of the art in the literature. Namely, if governing parties representing the economic right opt for Keynesian measures and opposition parties representing the economic left advocate neoliberal ones; it implies that the influence of the sovereign debt crisis was stronger than the impact of the basic economic orientation of a party and its governing status.

Methodological approach of this study

This section of the chapter presents the research design of the empirical analysis. The analysis was conducted in two stages: the first stage concerned the analysis of parliamentary plenary debates devoted to the increased budgetary capacity of the EFSF. That data helped to establish *how* parliamentary parties positioned themselves on anti-crisis measures (defined as preference for Keynesian or neoliberal anti-crisis policies). These positions constitute here the outcome of the analysis (the dependent variable). The goal of the second stage was to explain *why* certain parties opted either for Keynesian or neoliberal measures. In order to do so, various conditions (independent variables) were tested by means of the QCA crisp-set analysis.

The selection of states was based on their financial position operationalized as credit rating, based on the Standard & Poor data from autumn 2011. As a consequence, the analyzed euro states represent the following categories: triple-A group (Austria, France and Germany), mid-rating (Belgium and Slovenia), bailout likely (Spain) and bailout states (Ireland and Greece). It was assumed that the financial position of a state may have an impact on MPs' choices regarding the macroeconomic policy in the eurozone; hence, it would be a mistake to concentrate either on economically 'well-performing' or 'under-performing' states.

Methodological approach, step one: discourse analysis of plenary parliamentary debates

The outcome (the dependent variable) of the analysis is defined as *a position of a parliamentary party on anti-crisis measures* (neoliberal or Keynesian macroeconomic policies). The conditions (independent variables) tested in this study were: (1) economic orientation of a political party (left or right), (2) membership in a government or opposition and (3) receipt of a bailout.

In order to establish *how* parliamentary parties positioned themselves on economic anti-crisis measures, the empirical inference was based on national plenary parliamentary debates. The texts of the plenary debates were obtained from the publically accessible online archives of national parliaments. The analyzed debates took place between July and October 2011.[3]

As many authors noted (Wodak and van Dijk, 2000; Crespy and Gajewska, 2010; Wendler, 2011) parliamentary debates account most directly for the policy output. During plenary sessions MPs (or MEPs) explain their official stance on the debated legislation and engage in a discussion with other MPs. Their speeches reach not only the audience gathered in a plenary session but also their constituencies that follow the debate through the media. As Wodak and van Dijk (2000: 13) noted:

> Among the many genres of political discourse, (. . .) parliamentary debates symbolize democratic discussion, decision-making and power. (. . .) Parliamentary debates feature opinions based on different ideologies, and formulated against the background of different interests as represented by members of parliament (MPs) of different political parties.

The analyzed plenary parliamentary debates were devoted to the approval of the increased budgetary capacity of the European Financial Stability Facility (EFSF) that took place in autumn 2011. The EFSF is a temporary bailout fund established by the governments of the eurozone in order to provide financial assistance to the eurozone states. Acquisition of loans from the EFSF is based on strong conditionality. Each state that applies for a loan has to sign a Memorandum of Understanding (MoE) specifying where the loan should be invested and what kinds of policy measures have to be implemented (i.e. cuts in public spending). Implementation of the MoE is supervised by external bodies (the Troika), not only national ministries. As a consequence, a Memorandum of Understanding became a tool of implementing austerity measures in euro states receiving a bailout.

Why these debates? First, in autumn 2011 it was already possible for the MPs to evaluate the efficiency of the by now implemented anti-crisis measures. At the outburst of the eurozone crisis (spring 2010) political parties were under a strong time pressure to undertake preventive measures. Therefore, there was little space for an in-depth deliberation in parliaments. Additionally, in autumn 2011 MPs were also able to debate and evaluate the introduced anti-crisis measures from a perspective of one year. In this sense, their position was advantaged because they had a better knowledge regarding the reactions of financial markets to the introduced measures. Second, in autumn 2011, the lending power of the EFSF was doubled (from 240 billion euro to 440 billion euro) and with that the risks of contributing states also increased significantly. A default of one – or more – bailout states would impose higher financial burdens on contributing states. As a consequence, anti-crisis policies were placed high on national legislators' agendas.

For the sake of comparability, the analysis covered lower chambers only. This is because some states in the sample have a bicameral whereas others a unicameral parliamentary system. Furthermore, as a rule, these are lower chambers that are more engaged in EU politics than the upper chamber (Senate). For that reason one can expect that arguments voiced in lower chambers give a thorough and representative account of how parliamentary parties of a given state position themselves on EU issues.

The analysis was conducted with help of the Atlas.ti software which allows qualitative and quantitative discourse analysis to be conducted. The plenary debates were analyzed first in a qualitative manner. The unit of the analysis was an individual statement of an MP voiced during a plenary session. Each speech-act can contain more than one statement: in principle, MPs provide various grounds (justifications) in favour of a specific macroeconomic policy during their speech-time. The basic questions guiding the analysis of plenary debates were as follows: has a particular MP voiced support for a specific macroeconomic measure to be applied in the eurozone as an anti-crisis strategy? Can we classify that measure – with full certainty – as either Keynesian or neoliberal? Regarding the technical side of the analysis, only the relevant statements were coded. Within each statement the following elements were identified: (1) an actor being the author of the statement classified according to her political affiliation, (2) direction of the statement (e.g. was it a supportive statement?), (3) general type of a macroeconomic measure: was it a neoliberal or a Keynesian measure? and (4) exact policy instrument proposed (e.g. austerity during the economic downturn). If a certain measure or desired policy outcome could not be clearly associated with neoliberal or Keynesian approach, it was not coded. Finally, when the coding was completed, the data were merged on the party level.

In most cases identification of neoliberal or Keynesian measures did not pose significant difficulties. MPs who were advocating a neoliberal way out of crisis mainly concentrated on the economic necessity of austerity during the economic downturn.[4] Frequently they used a metaphor of a family whose spending became higher than the income. They would propose an 'obvious' solution to the problem, namely, a reduction of expenses during the economic crisis, for example:

> *The most important word is austerity. I studied economics in UCC, although not to any particular PhD level, and austerity is effectively*

the ability to balance our books. It applies to every household and to every business, and over time in the international community it must apply to individual states. No matter what happens in the world around us, our economy must arrive at a point where we are austere. It is being used as a negative term, but the reality is that we must bring in what we pay out to sustain our economic development.[5]

The advocates of neoliberal measures would also claim it is dangerous to increase public spending in times of crisis.[6] In the view of these MPs, public investment during economic crisis does not generate growth. Rather, it will increase the public debt and further undermine states' credibility on the market.

On the other hand, most Keynesians recommended states' interventionism as a generally effective way out of crisis. These MPs would often note that – historically – Keynesianism was successful in helping the US economy to recover from the Great Depression. Furthermore, in their view, the Keynesian approach is more effective in preventing the growth of unemployment because governments' spending helps to create work-places. These MPs would advocate an introduction of a fiscal stimulus for the eurozone states with financial difficulties. There were also MPs who pointed to a failure of the by now implemented neoliberal measures. These MPs would advocate the Keynesian approach as a viable alternative which eurozone states should try:

> *The problem is that you stick to a mistaken approach (neoliberal). These measures (. . .) are totally unsuitable because they undermine any economic recovery by compressing purchasing power.*[7]

Methodological approach, step two: QCA crisp-set analysis

In order to analyze the impact of various conditions (independent variables) on political parties' positioning on anti-crisis measures, the chapter employs the Qualitative Comparative Analysis (QCA) developed by Charles Ragin (Ragin, 1987; Schneider and Wagemann, 2007; Rihoux and Ragin, 2009). The empirical analysis presented in this chapter was conducted with help of the software fsQCA 2.0.[8] In general, the QCA is a configurational comparative analysis identifying combinations of conditions that are necessary or sufficient for a certain outcome.

Given the goal of the research and the nature of the explanatory factors, the chapter employs the crisp-set approach (csQCA). The crisp-set analysis is based on Boolean Algebra which implies that each case has a clearly defined 'membership': it is either 'fully in' or 'fully out'. That distinguishes the crisp-set approach from the fuzzy set approach in which cases can display a 'partial membership', for instance, unconsolidated democracies are not 'fully' democratic. As a consequence, crisp-set approach is more suitable for variables which account for the *difference in kind* (i.e. a party can be either in the government or in the opposition, neither both nor 'partially' in the opposition or partially in the government) rather than the *difference in degree* (i.e. how democratic a state is). Nonetheless, certain variables can be operationalized in both ways, depending on the goal of the analysis. Finally, the crisp-set approach cannot be used interchangeably with regression analysis: first, the QCA approach is most adequate for medium-size research designs and, second, there is no lineal relationship between conditions and the outcome but rather an impact of presence or absence of certain conditions.

The QCA approach is concerned not only with presence but also absence of certain conditions, which is a very important element of this analysis. For instance, we can investigate whether the absence of bailout has an effect on political parties' positioning.

The conditions tested in the QCA model were extracted mostly from the PIREDEU database and operationalized in a dichotomous way.[9] They were: (1) economic orientation of a party operationalized in a dichotomous way as left or right (PIREDEU: 'economic left or right'), (2) membership in a government or opposition during the period of the analysis (European Election Database) and (3) receipt of a bailout during the period of the analysis (EurActive information service).[10]

In an ideal case the explanatory model should cover all the analyzed parliamentary parties. However, that was impossible. The empirical dataset was too diverse: there were parties that opted for neoliberal or Keynesian anti-crisis measures (25 parties), but also 5 parties that were internally divided on that issue, meaning that some MPs within these parties opted for neoliberal measures whereas others for Keynesian ones. Since the data were merged on party level, these parties could not be classified as *either* neoliberal *or* Keynesian, but both. Finally, 14 parties did not position themselves at all or their macroeconomic positions could not be classified with the whole certainty. As a consequence, there were two distinct criteria that logically differentiated the cases: first, whether a parliamentary party positioned itself *at all* on anti-crisis measures and, second, which anti-crisis measures they opted for (given that they positioned themselves). For that reason the analyzed cases were clustered into three groups: (1) parties that positioned themselves, (2) parties with double positioning and (3) parties with no positioning. Only the first group of cases was applied to the QCA model, the second and the third groups were analyzed qualitatively.

Empirical evidence

This section of the chapter presents the empirical findings. It is divided into three sub-sections, the first one presenting the analysis of the positioned parties (the QCA crisp-set model), and the second one presenting the qualitative analysis of parties with 'double positioning' and parties that had not positioned themselves. The third section offers an interpretation of the findings in the light of the tested hypotheses.

Positioned parties: evidence from the crisp-set QCA analysis

The analysis of necessary conditions demonstrated that the condition 'economic left' had the highest consistency and coverage (0.909091 and 0.833333) in accounting for the presence of the outcome (Keynesian positioning). This means that, first, almost 90 percent of parties opting for Keynesian measures represented the economic left. Second, 83 percent of parties representing 'economic left' opted for Keynesian measures. In comparison, the condition 'membership in the opposition' had a consistency value of 0.909091 but the coverage of only 0.588235. The third condition, 'receipt of a bailout' had the lowest consistency value of 0.454545 but the highest coverage: 1.0 which implies that *all* parties from states that received a bailout opted for Keynesian measures only.

The QCA analysis identified three casual paths of support for Keynesian anti-crisis measures. The conditions for the presence of Keynesian positioning were: (1) left-wing economic orientation AND (2) membership in the opposition AND (3) receipt of a bailout (see Table 6.2). The results present the complex solution (see Table 6.3). The first group of parties supporting Keynesian anti-crisis measures was characterized by the combination of two conditions: 'economic left-wing orientation' AND 'membership in the

Table 6.2 Truth table, presence of the outcome (Keynesian positioning)

Conditions			Outcome	Raw consistency
gov	right	bailout	k	
0	1	0	0	0
0	0	0	1	1
1	1	0	0	0
0	0	1	1	1
1	0	0	0	0
0	1	1	1	1
1	0	1	1	1

Source: Author

102 *Macroeconomic preferences*

Table 6.3 Complex solution: presence of the outcome (Keynesian positioning)

Configuration	Raw coverage	Unique coverage	Consistency	Cases (parties)
~right*~gov	0.818182	0.545455	1.000.000	SPD (1,1), Linke (1,1), Socialists (1,1), KKE (1,1), Syriza (1,1), PS-Belgium (1,1), IU (1,1), ERC (1,1), GDR (1,1)
bailout*~gov	0.363636	0.090909	1.000.000	Socialists (1,1), KKE (1,1), ND (1,1), Syriza (1,1)
bailout*~right	0.363636	0.090909	1.000.000	Lab (1,1), Socialists (1,1), KKE (1,1), Syriza (1,1)

solution coverage: 1.000000
solution consistency: 1.000000

Source: Author

opposition'. These parties were: SDP (Germany), Linke (Germany), Socialists (Ireland), KKE (Greece), Syriza (Greece), PS (Belgium), IU (Spain), ERC, GDR (France). 54 percent of all the cases were characterized *exclusively* by that pattern. The second group was characterized by the combination 'receipt of a bailout' AND 'membership in the opposition' whereas the third one by 'receipt of a bailout' AND 'economic left-wing orientation'. The parties belonging to the second pattern were: Socialists, KKE, ND, Syriza. The third group was composed of: Labour, Socialists, KKE and Syriza.

The analysis of necessary conditions for neoliberal positioning of parliamentary parties demonstrated that the highest consistency and coverage had the condition 'right-wing orientation' (0.857143 and 0.923077). This means that, first, 86 percent of parties opting for neoliberal measures represented the economic right. Second, 92 percent of parties representing the 'economic right' opted for neoliberal anti-crisis measures. The condition 'membership in the government' had a consistency score of 0.500000 and coverage of 0.875000 whereas 'absence of a bailout' 1.00000 and 0.700000. In the latter case the consistency result indicated that *all* parties opting for neoliberal measures belong to non-bailout states.

The QCA model proposed two casual paths explaining the neoliberal positioning of parties: first one composed of conditions 'absence of a bailout' AND 'economic right' and the second one also composed of two conditions 'absence of a bailout' AND 'membership in the government' (see Tables 6.4 and 6.5). The first casual path had a stronger explanatory power: 86 percent of cases with that combination of conditions explained the neoliberal positioning. For the second explanatory path the raw coverage value was much lower, namely, 50 percent.

Table 6.4 Truth table: absence of the outcome (neoliberal positioning)

Conditions			Outcome	Raw consistency
gov	right	bailout	~k	
0	1	0	1	1
0	0	0	0	0
1	1	0	1	1
0	0	1	0	0
1	0	0	1	1
0	1	1	0	0
1	0	1	0	0

Source: Author

Table 6.5 Complex solution: absence of the outcome (neoliberal positioning)

Configuration	Raw coverage	Unique coverage	Consistency	Cases (parties)
~bailout*right	0.857143	0.500000	1.000.000	CDU (1,1), CSU (1,1), FDP (1,1,), OVP (1.1), FPO (1,1), N-VA (1,1), CD&V (1.1), VB (1,1), PP (1,1), CIU (1,1), UMP (1,1), NC (1,1)
~bailout*gov	0.500000	0.142857	1.000.000	CDU (1,1), CSU (1,1), FDP (1,1), OVP (1,1), UMP (1,1), ZARES (1,1), Liberal Democracy (1,1)

solution coverage: 1.000000
solution consistency: 1.000000

Source: Author

Parties with 'double' positioning and the 'salient' ones

The five parties that were internally divided, that is, whose MPs supported both neoliberal and Keynesian measures belonged, with one exception (the German Green party), to states that had received a bailout by the time of the analysis (Greece and Ireland). The internally divided parties were: Greens (Germany), FG (Ireland), SF (Ireland), FF (Ireland) and PASOK (Greece). Parties with 'double positioning' demonstrate that receipt of a bailout is likely to generate substantial internal conflicts in parliamentary parties. In that group MPs opted for Keynesian anti-crisis measures *despite* the economic stance of their party or membership in the government.

The 14 political parties that did not position themselves at all belonged, with two exceptions, to the opposition parties. These were both left- and right-wing parties from the non-bailout and bailout states: PSOE (Spain), Slovenian National Party (Slovenia), Slovenian Democratic Party (Slovenia), DeSUS (Slovenia), PS-France (France), MR (France), sp.a (Belgium), Open Vld (Belgium), DIMAR (Greece), DISY (Greece), People Before Profit (Ireland), LAOS (Greece), SD (Slovenia), Slovenian Peoples Party (Slovenia).

Interpretation of the results

The empirical findings based on the QCA analysis reveals two distinct mechanisms accounting for political parties' positioning: the first one confirms the 'state of the art' hypothesis according to which macroeconomic policy outcomes depend on the economic stance of the governing party: whereas parties representing the economic left advocate Keynesian macroeconomic measures, right-wing parties opt for neoliberal ones.

However, the second mechanism challenges the first account. It reveals a crisis-specific logic of positioning in which a receipt of a bailout influences parliamentary parties' choices of macroeconomic anti-crisis measures. In particular, parties from states which received a bailout support Keynesian anti-crisis measures despite their right-wing economic orientation or membership in the government. That mechanism also demonstrates that in a shared currency system bailout and creditor states are guided by a different logic. Bailout states demonstrate contestation of neoliberal anti-crisis measures which are implemented in their states. On the contrary, creditor states were not affected by a crisis-specific logic of positioning: they positioned themselves according to their general economic stance. For instance, left-wing parties in creditor states did not opt for neoliberal measures, which would constitute a strong case for crisis-specific positioning among creditor states.

The following paragraphs analyze the empirical findings in more detail. Regarding the first – ideology-based – hypothesis, parliamentary parties opted for Keynesian positioning predominantly due to ideological reasons. The dominant explanatory pattern comprised the combination of two conditions: 'economic left' AND 'membership in the opposition'. Nonetheless, as the analysis of necessary conditions demonstrated, 'economic left' had a much higher consistency and coverage than 'membership in the opposition'. In particular, there was only one party, ND in Greece, which opted for Keynesian measures despite being classified as economically right-wing party. Otherwise, Keynesian positioning was chosen by parties representing the economic left.

The conflict of interest between creditors and debtors constituted the second pattern explaining the Keynesian positioning. The effects of that conflict are most visible if we analyze together the results of the QCA analysis and the qualitative findings regarding parties with double positioning. The QCA model demonstrates that whenever 'receipt of bailout' was present as a condition, a party would opt for Keynesian anti-crisis measures. Nonetheless, these are not 'strong cases' supporting the logic of creditors' and debtors' interest. With two exceptions, all the parties concerned represented the economic left and belonged to the opposition. Hence, we cannot exclude the possibility that these parties would choose Keynesian measures also in the absence of a bailout. On the other hand, if we take into consideration the analysis of parties with double positioning, we can observe an interesting pattern. Apparently, bailout *does* play a role for it leads to internal splits in parties which otherwise would be likely to opt for neoliberal measures, that is, parties representing the economic right or the governing parties.

Neoliberal positioning was explained by two patterns: the first one being the 'absence of a bailout' AND 'economic right' and the second being the 'absence of a bailout' AND 'membership in the government'. The first pattern was clearly dominant, covering 86 percent of cases in which neoliberal positioning was chosen. There is no strong evidence that the choice of neoliberal measures reflected the conflict of interests between creditors and debtors. Namely, there are only two parties that represent the 'economic left' but who opted nonetheless for neoliberal measures (Liberal Democracy and ZARES in Slovenia). However, both of these parties belonged to the government, which can also imply that their choice of anti-crisis measures was related to that factor. As a consequence, similarly to Keynesian positioning, the choice of neoliberal anti-crisis measures was predominantly ideology-based. Furthermore, whereas presence of a bailout had an effect on political parties' macroeconomic choices (the second pattern accounting for Keynesian positioning), there is no evidence that the absence of a bailout had an effect on neoliberal positioning.

Regarding the neoliberal positioning, the first group of political parties is characterized by the absence of a bailout, economic right and membership in the governing majority. The second group displays only one difference; namely, affiliation to the opposition. Analyzing both patterns together, one can infer that affiliation to the governing majority or opposition was not decisive for a political party to opt for neoliberal measures. As a consequence, we can rule out the impact of institutional aspects. Rather, these were two other factors that account for the choice of neoliberal measures: right-wing orientation and the absence of a bailout. However, since all cases in the neoliberal group are characterized by both attributes (absence of a bailout and economic right), it is impossible to argue whether the 'absence of a bailout' or 'economic right' had more impact on their decision.

The 'salience' of the opposition parties can be interpreted in various ways. First, parties in non-bailout states could have been indifferent to the topic. Second, these parties may have been lacking a necessary expertise to engage in the discussion. After all, it should not be forgotten that the eurozone crisis forced national parliaments to engage with issues which until now remained outside their major focus. Third, their salience could be strategic given the fact that national political parties use European issues for domestic politics. However, 'salience' of governing parties, here PSOE and the DeSUS, may suggest a different logic. These two parties represented the economic left. Under these conditions their 'salience' was a strategy of accommodating the internal conflict with which the parties were confronted. Support of Keynesian measures would imply a change of the by now adopted neoliberal anti-crisis policy.

Conclusions

The major goal of this chapter was to establish *why* national parliamentary parties in the eurozone states opted either for neoliberal or Keynesian anti-crisis measures to be implemented in the bailout states. Drawing on the combination of parliamentary debates' analysis and the Qualitative Comparative Analysis (QCA) the chapter tested the impact of the following factors on parties' positioning: the economic orientation of a party, conflicting interests between creditors and debtors and the cleavage between the government and the opposition.

The findings presented in this chapter demonstrate that financial interdependence of states in the shared currency realm generated a new mechanism guiding political parties' positioning on macroeconomic policies. As the empirical data demonstrated, parties from states that received a bailout are particularly prone to propose macroeconomic measures reflecting their interests as debtor states. Namely, despite their right-wing economic orientation or membership in the government, parliamentary parties from the bailout states opted for Keynesian measures. This finding demonstrates that the mechanisms of political parties' positioning in shared currency systems are more complex than in single currency systems.

The second mechanism of political parties' positioning confirmed the existing knowledge based on the analysis of single currency systems. According to the literature macroeconomic policy outcomes depend on the economic stance of the governing party: whereas parties representing the economic left advocate Keynesian macroeconomic measures, right-wing parties opt for neoliberal ones. That mechanism was clearly dominant among creditor states in which parliamentary parties were not affected by a crisis-specific logic of positioning.

The empirical findings presented in this chapter suggest two avenues for further research. First, it remains to be investigated why a significant group of parliamentary parties decided not to position themselves on macroeconomic measures: was it a 'strategic' decision or maybe that party lacked expertise or interest in that matter? Examination of that issue would certainly widen our knowledge on national parliamentary parties' involvement in the EU politics. The second avenue for further research concerns a longitude comparative analysis of macroeconomic policy choices by national parties in the EU. It remains to be investigated deeper which factors influence parties' positions on macroeconomic policies (in the national and in the EU context) and how stable these positions remain over a longer period of time.

Notes

1 This book chapter has been published in a slightly modified form in the *Journal of European Public Policy*, for comparison see: Maatsch, A. (2014). 'Are We All Austerians Now? An Analysis of National Parliamentary Parties' Positioning on Anti-Crisis Measures in the Eurozone'. *Journal of European Public Policy*, 21(1), 95–115.
2 In the first version of the analysis the impact of Euroscepticism was also tested (based on the PIREDEU codes 'Europe, EC/EU' positive and negative and 'Transfer of power to the EU' positive and negative). The variable was dropped because it did not really account for positioning of parties.
3 Germany (Bundestag: 08.09.2011, 29.09.2011), Austria (Nationalrat: 30.09.2011), Ireland (Dail Eireann: 20.09.2011, 21.09.2011), France (Assemblée Nationale 06/07.09.2011), Slovenia (Drzavni Zbor: 19.09.2011), Belgium (la Chambre des Representants: 29.08.2011, 09.09.2011, 13.09.2011), Greece (Hellenic Parliament: 20.09.2011, 22.09.09.2011, 27.09.2011), Spain (Congreso de los Diputados: 15.09.2011).
4 Keynesians are not against austerity measures as such but they recommend that they be implemented during the period of economic growth.
5 Fine Gael (Ireland), 21.09.2011.
6 That measure is recommended by Keynesians.
7 GDR (France), 06.09.2011.
8 http://www.compasss.org
9 http://www.piredeu.eu/DC/index2.asp
10 The PIREDEU database is accessible online after prior registration (URL: http://www.piredeu.eu/DC/index2.asp). The data is available in the Excess or Excel format. In the PIREDEU database party positions were usually coded on a 10-point scale which allows transforming various 'codes' or 'indexes' both into fuzzy or dichotomous variables. Few recently established parliamentary parties were not covered by the PIREDEU database, namely, People Before Profit (Ireland) or GDR (France). Their economic stance (left–right) was established on the basis of their current party programmes (the method employed in the PIREDEU project).

7 Conclusions

Have national parliaments been reduced to mere talking shops or are they truly deliberative bodies involved in the reform of European economic governance? In other words, are national parliaments nothing more than venues for superficial discussion? Have MPs become devoid of formal powers and motivation to perform their constitutional roles? Or, on the contrary, have they successfully carried out their legislative, control and representative functions? Finally, does the reform period with which we are concerned constitute only a brief interruption in the Lisbon Process or is it something new? In order to answer these questions we evaluated the performance of national parliaments during the European financial crisis in terms of the three major functions of national parliaments, namely, law-making competences – ratification of international agreements – government scrutiny and representation.

The core of the empirical analysis presented in this book concern national parliaments' activities during the reform of European economic governance. It focusses on parliaments' involvement in the approval (or ratification) of the following measures: the European Financial Stability Facility (a temporary bailout fund) and the increase of its budgetary capacity that followed a few months later, ratification of the European Stability Mechanism (the permanent bailout fund) and ratification of the Treaty on Stability, Coordination and Governance in the Economic and Monetary Union, also referred to as the Fiscal Compact. The analysis is embedded in a broader narrative presenting various factors recognized as direct or indirect causes of the eurozone crisis, such as the global financial meltdown in 2008. The empirical analysis closes in mid-2013 when ratification of the Fiscal Compact was completed.

In this book the activities of national parliament are analyzed in a range of dimensions. First, the book provides a comparative analysis of formal procedures employed at the national level in order to approve the anti-crisis measures under analysis (Chapter 3). The analysis examines the states in which the formal competences of national parliaments were limited and in what ways. Second, the book presents results from a comprehensive comparative analysis of parliamentary parties' voting behaviour on each of the anti-crisis measures analyzed (Chapter 4). The third dimension of the investigation is a comparative qualitative discourse analysis of national parliamentary parties' discourses justifying their voting (Chapter 5). Fourth, the study analyzes parliamentary parties' preferences with respect to 'Keynesian' or neoliberal macroeconomic measures (Chapter 6).

Given the book's multi-dimensional analytical perspective, the study employs a variety of research methods: comparative legal analysis (formal approval procedures) (Chapter 3); statistical analysis of voting outcomes (Chapter 4); qualitative discourse analysis (Chapter 5); and Qualitative Comparative Analysis (QCA) to study macroeconomic preferences (Chapter 6). Whereas the analysis of formal procedures and voting behaviour covered all member states of the eurozone, discourse analysis was limited to the following states: Austria, Belgium, France, Germany, Greece, Ireland, Luxembourg, the Netherlands, Slovakia, Slovenia and Spain.

Approval of anti-crisis measures

The empirical analysis demonstrates that national parliaments' formal powers with regard to the approval of anti-crisis measures were affected by three different types of asymmetry: application of fast-track procedures and mergers, national supreme or constitutional court activities and an international asymmetry concerning the substantive equality of national parliaments.

First, at the domestic level, governments of debtor states restricted parliaments' powers through fast-track procedures and mergers, which curtailed not only parliamentary control but also deliberation (see Chapter 3 for more details). For instance, in some states emergency legislation made it possible to eliminate plenary debates entirely, leaving only voting, while in other states the usual number of plenary debates was reduced. There were also 'mergers', whereby two or more legislative acts were combined and presented for parliamentary debate and voting as one package.

Fast-track procedures are not inherently undemocratic. In general, emergency legislation is envisaged for situations in which it is justifiable to shorten the usual legislative procedures, such as natural disasters. In order to control the use of fast-track procedures, states stipulate the circumstances in which emergency legislation can be applied. Given the lack of harmonization of these practices, there is a lot of variation among European states. For instance, some states restrict national parliaments' powers only to a minor extent, for instance, limiting the usual number of plenary debates.

However, there are states in which the emergency legislation makes it possible to circumvent national parliaments entirely. Furthermore, in some states emergency legislation can be extended to a broader range of policies than in other states. As a result, due to different national constitutional orders, national parliaments do not enjoy equally generous democratic arrangements in each EU member state (De Witte, 2010).

Empirical analysis of anti-crisis measures' approval procedures in each member state of the eurozone demonstrates that the impact of national parliaments was limited and highly asymmetrical. Southern European parliaments' powers were more constrained than their northern European counterparts. The states that approved anti-crisis measures *without* employing any fast-track procedure or merger were: Belgium, Austria, Estonia, Finland, Germany, Ireland, Luxembourg, Slovakia and Slovenia. With the exception of Ireland, all the states belong to the group of so-called 'creditors'. States that approved European anti-crisis measures either with fast-track procedures or mergers were: Spain, France, Cyprus, Greece, Italy, Malta, Netherlands and Portugal. In the second group the outliers are France and the Netherlands.

The ratification procedures of the Fiscal Compact varied significantly across states. The observed practices differed with regard to the degree of national parliaments' involvement or influence. In a number of states, voting on particular anti-crisis measures was dispensed with: in Cyprus (EFSF-2 and the Fiscal Compact), Greece (EFSF-1), Italy (EFSF-1 and EFSF-2), the Netherlands (EFSF-1) and Portugal (EFSF-2). Plenary debate was eschewed entirely in the following states: Spain (EFSF-1 and EFSF-2, Fiscal Compact), Cyprus (EFSF-2, Fiscal Compact), Greece (EFSF-1) and the Netherlands (EFSF-2). In France the usual number of plenary debates was reduced from three to one (the EFSF-1, EFSF-2, ESM and the Fiscal Compact).

Mergers took place in the following states: Spain (ESM and Article 136 TFEU), France (EFSF-1 was merged with the budget bill and the ESM Treaty was merged with Article 136 TFEU), Greece (EFSF-2 was merged with the law on property tax and bank supervision, the ESM Treaty was merged with Article 136 TFEU and the Fiscal Compact), Italy (Article 136 TFEU, ESM, Fiscal Compact), Malta (ESM merged with Article 136 TFEU), the Netherlands (EFSF-2 with the budgetary law, ESM with Article 136 TFEU) and Portugal (ESM and Article 136 TFEU).

An extreme merger that severely constrained the national parliament's powers occurred in Greece, where ratification of the ESM Treaty was merged with the revision of Article 136(3), as well as ratification of the Fiscal Compact and the budgetary balanced rule. Parliamentarians had only one plenary debate and one vote at their disposal to approve – or reject – the whole legislative package. A further concern relates to the time available for discussion. As a consequence, the analysis demonstrates that governments of bailout states used their available prerogatives in order to accelerate the legislative process and increase the likelihood of anti-crisis measures' being approved by limiting national parliaments' involvement.

The second asymmetry that influenced parliamentary competences in the approval of anti-crisis measures concerned national supreme or constitutional courts. Application of fast-track procedures depends to a large extent on constitutional courts that, in case of uncertainty, declare whether a particular application is constitutional. During the period of the reform, only the German Constitutional Court (BVG) clearly confirmed the powers of the German parliament (Bundestag). However, constitutional and supreme courts in bailout states, in which fast-track procedures were applied the most, did not declare their extensive application to be unconstitutional (see Chapter 3 for more details). In Spain the rulings of the Constitutional Court, which, for example, recognized the application of a fast-track procedure to labour law reform, met with severe criticism from constitutional lawyers.

Finally, the third asymmetry concerns substantive inequalities. According to the law all national parliaments of the EU member states are formally equal; however, for various reasons parliaments can become constrained in the exercise of their competences. During the reform of European economic governance the national parliaments of bailout states were afflicted by a loss of substantive equality. In that process, the award of bailout loans was conditioned on ratification of the Fiscal Compact and introduction of the balanced budget rule into domestic legislation. That condition constrained national parliaments in exercising their powers: practically speaking, parliaments in bailout states could neither reject the Fiscal Compact nor delay the ratification process. Otherwise they risked losing financial aid.

In sum, the analysis of asymmetries affecting national parliaments' formal powers in approving anti-crisis measures demonstrates a gap between creditor and bailout states. In particular, in contrast to creditor states, parliaments of bailout states were restricted in their formal competences through extensive application of fast-track procedures and mergers, constitutional or supreme court positions and the lack of substantive equality.

Control and representative functions

How did national parliaments carry out their control and representative functions? Were MPs well-prepared to debate the subsequent anti-crisis measures? How diverse were their arguments and evaluations? Did parliamentary parties manage to debate and provide various policy options to their voters? Did parliamentary parties represent their constituencies' preferences in their voting behaviour and plenary debates?

In order to evaluate national parliaments' control and representative functions during the reform of European economic governance the empirical analysis presented in this book focusses on parliamentary parties' voting behaviour on all anti-crisis measures, MPs' discourses – revealing their evaluations of anti-crisis measures – and their macroeconomic preferences. Obviously, formal competences also mattered. In particular, if a given measure is introduced with a fast-track procedure that eliminates or reduces the usual number of plenary debates, national parliaments are restricted in the exercise of control and representative functions, which are then carried out predominantly discursively.

Voting by parliamentary parties is recognized as the major means of representing constituencies' interests. Parliamentary parties, seeking re-election, tend to vote according to the perceived preferences of their constituencies. Parliamentary parties' orientation towards voters' interests is usually referred to in the literature as *responsiveness* (Mair, 2009, 2011). However, due to various factors, such as international obligations, national parliamentary parties are sometimes obliged to vote contrary to the preferences of their constituencies.

The reform of European economic governance is a particularly good topic for examining how parliamentary parties perform their representative functions. The empirical analysis covers vote outcomes on the European Financial Stability Facility (EFSF) (both the establishment of the fund and the increase of its budgetary capacity), the European Stability Mechanism (ESM) and the Fiscal Compact. The analysis covered all eurozone members. The basis of the analysis was defined as a vote by a party on a particular measure. The sample comprised 402 observations. The empirical analysis was based on a set of logit models testing the impact of the following factors: governing status, the economic left–right cleavage, position on EU integration, impact of public opinion (measured by trust in national and EU institutions and evaluation of their crisis-solving capacity), the impact of the conflict between debtor and creditor states as well as the impact of formal ratification procedures.

The analysis demonstrates that the voting of governing and opposition parties exhibit entirely different patterns. First, none of the governing parties in the sample voted against the anti-crisis measures analyzed, while opposition parties voted in favour or against. The broad support of governing parties for all the anti-crisis measures has been attributed to international *responsibility* (Mair, 2009, 2011). Given the fact that the analyzed anti-crisis measures required the unanimous approval of all states (or 'special' majorities), governing parties were aware that a failure by their state to ratify them could put the whole reform process on hold.

Conclusions 113

The major factor explaining opposition parties' vote outcomes was their position on the EU. In particular, Eurosceptic opposition parties opposed anti-crisis measures, whereas pro-EU opposition parties supported them. In contrast to governing parties, opposition parties' voting behaviour was more *responsive* to their voters' preferences. In particular, in states where voters' trust in their governments was high, opposition parties were more likely to vote in favour of anti-crisis measures. On the contrary, opposition parties were more prone to vote against anti-crisis measures if voters' trust in national parliaments was high. Finally, the analysis also demonstrates that the higher the public trust in the capacity of the EU to solve the financial crisis, the more likely were the opposition parties to vote in favour of anti-crisis measures. As a result, opposition parties have clearly better managed to represent voters' preferences than governing parties.

In order to fully accomplish the control and representative functions, parliamentary parties are also expected to provide policy options that take into consideration dominant cleavages in their societies. In other words, parliamentary parties are able to establish a link between voters and the debated issue if their voting behaviour – but also discourses – considers their constituencies' preferences. Given that, it should be noted that opposition parties only partially failed in their task. The empirical analysis demonstrates that national parliamentary parties failed to incorporate the economic dimension into their voting behaviour. The model also tested the impact of the radical left and right positions but these proved to be irrelevant.

Instead, parties' voting patterns were explained predominantly by their position on the European Union. By the same token, the analysis confirms the thesis that political parties' behaviour within European economic governance is structured by the conflict over identity rather than by redistribution (Hooghe and Marks, 2008). Finally, the majority of governing and opposition parties reached an internal consensus on anti-crisis measures and voted unanimously in favour of or against them. The finding confirms that the analyzed parties managed to present unitary positions even in a highly controversial policy area such as European economic governance.

Obviously, it must be noted that the recognition of *international responsibility* by parliamentary parties is not inherently undemocratic. In fact, respect for international agreements and willingness to compromise are important components of international politics. Ideally, parliamentary parties should balance *international responsibility* with *responsiveness* towards voters' preferences. However, as the reform of European economic governance demonstrates, adhering to these two principles can sometimes be very difficult.

Political discourses and, more specifically, plenary debates are a crucial source of inference regarding the control and representative functions of national parliamentary parties. At the general level the empirical analysis established that parliamentary parties remained well-informed about the particularities of each debated institutional measure, which was not an easy task given the enormous time pressure. Furthermore, the vast majority of parliamentary parties clearly established and articulated their positions, which differed significantly. Finally, the analysis demonstrated that some parties tended to be more critical in their discourses than in their voting behaviour. Apparently, plenary debates constituted an opportunity for parliamentary parties to raise their concerns and criticisms without endangering the outcome of the ratification process.

The analysis of plenary debates demonstrated that supporters of anti-crisis measures were divided into pragmatic and idealistic sub-groups. Pragmatic supporters, composed of governing parties, referred predominantly to particularistic national economic interests. In contrast, idealistic supporters, represented by mainstream opposition parties, more frequently employed ethical arguments referring to the political value of the European Union and of the European integration process as such. Although the reforms – and particularly the establishment of the bailout fund – implied a basic solidarity among member states, supporters of the reforms decided not to employ moral arguments (see also Closa and Maatsch, 2014). Rather, it was far more common among the supporters to refer to 'the spirit of positive conditionality' inspiring institutional reform in general.

Opponents of anti-crisis measures were also composed of two distinct sub-groups: nationalists and anti-austerians. Both groups consisted of Eurosceptic parties, but the nationalists were represented by the right-wing Eurosceptic parties and anti-austerians by the left-wing Eurosceptics. Nationalists rejected the anti-crisis measures under analysis, pointing predominantly to national economic or political interests. They also justified their position with treaty articles forbidding bailouts. In their narrative, responsibility for the crisis is attributed to southern European states. By contrast, anti-austerians rejected the relevant measures on the grounds of solidarity. These parties argued that austerity violates the principle of solidarity because the policy burdens ordinary people with the costs of the crisis. Furthermore, anti-austerians voiced doubts whether austerity in general is likely to generate growth and employment in southern Europe.

The empirical analysis also focussed on the macroeconomic preferences of parliamentary parties. During the reform of European economic governance a parallel debate between Keynesian and neoliberal economists unfolded in the public sphere. Plenary debates devoted to ratification of anti-crisis measures became an opportunity for parliamentary parties to engage with and contribute to that debate. Hence, the goal of the analysis became to establish which macroeconomic policies (neoliberal or Keynesian) parliamentary parties advocate in bailout states and why. The study tested the impact of the following factors on parties' positioning: economic orientation, conflicting interests between creditors and debtors, position on EU integration and cleavage between government and opposition.

The analysis demonstrates two patterns of parliamentary parties' positioning on macroeconomic policies. The first pattern reflected the well-established state of the art in the literature according to which the general economic orientation of a party (right- or left-wing) explains the choice of macroeconomic policies during a financial crisis. As a consequence, right-wing parties tend to opt for neoliberal measures, whereas left-wing parties go for Keynesian ones. That mechanism was clearly dominant among creditor states. The second mechanism reflected an entirely new logic. As the empirical data demonstrate, parties in states that received a bailout were particularly prone to advocate macroeconomic measures reflecting their interests as debtor states. Namely, despite their right-wing economic orientation or membership in the government, many parliamentary parties in bailout states revealed their preference for Keynesian measures.

The analysis demonstrated that in shared currency systems parties' macroeconomic policy preferences are influenced by not only the general left or right economic stance of a party but also their position as a debtor or a creditor. That finding generated further questions which still demand to be answered. First, it has to be verified whether parliamentary parties in bailout states opted strategically for Keynesian measures or whether their preference was ideologically motivated. Namely, further research should establish whether the recent experience with the financial crisis generally discouraged parliamentary parties in bailout states from applying neoliberal measures. Second, there are as yet no studies that demonstrate whether parties in bailout states differentiate between national and internationally-coordinated responses towards a financial crisis. In particular, it is unclear whether the same parties would propose Keynesian measures if they could cope with a financial crisis without needing a bailout loan.

Talking shop or deliberative body?

In a eurozone struggling with the effects of the financial crisis the conditions for parliamentary democracy have not been particularly favourable. According to Rodrik (2011), the principles of democracy and sovereignty have given way to the demands of financial markets. And these have rather expected *responsible* (Mair, 2009, 2011) than *responsive* behaviour from parliamentary parties. Governing parties, by voting in favour of each and every anti-crisis measure – often against the will of their own constituencies – clearly responded to the demands of financial markets.

Parliamentary democracy suffered most in bailout states, where the involvement of external non-elected actors in national budgetary matters prevented voters and parliamentary parties from holding decision-makers accountable. As a result, subsequent changes of governments, particularly in Greece, have not been able to produce a domestic policy change. Having signed Memorandums of Understanding, parties in bailout states lost their sovereign powers in budgetary matters and thus found it difficult to act upon their electoral promises regarding national budgets. These circumstances have proven to be particularly frustrating for voters, who quickly realized that their participation in popular elections is almost redundant.

The period of European economic governance's reform has proven to be particularly challenging for national parliaments. First and foremost, national parliaments' formal powers became restricted by national governments that frequently decided to approve anti-crisis measures with fast-track procedures. Fast-track procedures not only curbed parliaments' formal powers of approval but also indirectly influenced their discursive capacities as deliberative institutions. In particular, if a fast-track procedure reduced or eliminated the standard number of plenary debates, parliamentary parties were deprived of a necessary institutional framework to fulfil their representative and control functions.

However, the assessment of national parliaments' performance during the reform of European economic governance also depends on *how* MPs used their powers in order to approve anti-crisis measures, control their governments and represent and inform their voters. The comparative analysis of parliamentary parties' voting behaviour demonstrates that all governing parties prioritized international *responsibility* and supported – predominantly unanimously – every anti-crisis measure. Among opposition parties the most important factor was their position on European integration. In particular, whereas parties in favour of European integration supported anti-crisis measures, Eurosceptic parties voted against. In contrast to governing parties, opposition parties also voted more *responsively* with regard to their voters' preferences. However, the voting behaviour of political parties, both governing and opposition, was devoid of an economic dimension, meaning that parties representing the economic left or right have not voted differently. The absence of the economic left–right dimension in voting behaviour, so central to budgetary matters, can be recognized as an obstacle to domesticating reform of European economic governance at the national level. In other words, parliamentary parties failed to provide policy alternatives to voters with different macroeconomic preferences.

The discourse analysis conducted in this study focussed on two questions: first, how parliamentary parties justified their votes on anti-crisis measures and, second, which macroeconomic approaches (Keynesian or neoliberal) they favoured. Both parts of the analysis demonstrated that parliamentary parties were well-informed about the matters under discussion. It must be noted, however, that small (or regional) parties usually have not voiced their stance on macroeconomic approaches. Nonetheless, they justified why they voted in favour of or against anti-crisis measures discursively.

The two dimensions (government versus opposition and pro- versus anti-EU) structuring political conflicts in voting behaviour were reflected in discourses providing justifications for vote outcomes. In this way, national parliaments were oriented mainly towards cooperating with governments; they have not sought confrontation.

However, the analysis of parliamentary parties' discursive positioning on macroeconomic approaches (Keynesian or neoliberal) demonstrated that the major divide arose between left- and right-wing parties, as well as between parties in bailout and creditor states. The finding demonstrated that parliamentary parties were clearly more successful in accommodating relevant cleavages within their discourses rather than in their voting behaviour.

In general, the findings demonstrate that despite the limitation of formal powers and the prioritization of international responsibility among governing parties, national parliaments have not become mere talking shops. Given the fact that discourses played such a central role in the pursuit of control and representative functions, it remains desirable that parliamentary debates are not constrained in the future by extensive application of fast-track procedures.

Future challenge: national parliaments within the European semester

The reform of European economic governance constituted an extremely turbulent, but fairly short, period of time. The question emerges whether it has only been an interruption in the process initiated by the Treaty of Lisbon, promoting parliaments' empowerment or, on the contrary, a new trend? These questions require further research to examine national parliaments' performance within the newly established institutional framework of the European Semester.

The European Semester, in force since 2011, is an institutional instrument for preventive surveillance of economic and fiscal policies of EU member states. The goal of the instrument is to ensure 'closer coordination of economic policies and sustained convergence of the economic performance of the Member States'.[1] The mechanism enhances policy-coordination on macroeconomic and structural issues across all member states of the European Union. An important aspect of the mechanism is that national and fiscal policies of EU member states are assessed by the European Commission before they enter into force.

The legal basis of the European Semester is provided in the so-called six-pack composed of the following regulations and directives: Regulation 1175/2011 amending Regulation 1466/97: On the strengthening of the surveillance of budgetary positions and the surveillance and coordination of economic policies, Regulation 1177/2011 amending Regulation 1467/97: On speeding up and clarifying the implementation of the excessive deficit procedure, Regulation 1173/2011: On the effective enforcement of budgetary surveillance in the euro area, Directive 2011/85/EU: On requirements for budgetary frameworks of the Member States, Regulation 1176/2011: On the prevention and correction of macroeconomic imbalances, Regulation 1174/2011: On enforcement action to correct excessive macroeconomic imbalances in the euro area; and the two-pack composed of Regulation 473/2013: On common provisions for monitoring and assessing draft budgetary plans and ensuring the correction of excessive deficit of the Member States in the euro area and Regulation 472/2013: On the strengthening of economic and budgetary surveillance of Member States in the euro area experiencing or threatened with serious difficulties with respect to their financial stability. Furthermore, the European Semester also draws on Article 121 TFEU on the Broad Economic Policy Guidelines and Article 148 TFEU on the Employment Guidelines.

Studies focussing on formal procedures have already demonstrated that the institutional set-up of the European Semester does not limit the budgetary competences of national parliaments (Fasone, 2015). However, the question remains open how particular national parliaments are going to fulfil their role given the national and international asymmetries of power that are likely to persist in the future. In particular, as the literature demonstrates (Maatsch, 2017), some national parliaments enjoy stronger constitutional powers in budgetary matters than others. Therefore, these parliaments are more likely to play a prominent role in the European Semester. Furthermore, in the course of the reform of European economic governance the Commission's and the Council's powers in budgetary matters increased substantially. Among others, the Commission reviews national budgets and provides recommendations that have to be implemented by national parliaments. If these fail to comply with the new budgetary standards or recommendations concerning economic policies, the Commission can issue financial sanctions. As a result, the European

Semester disempowered national parliaments in their budgetary decision-making competences.

As already noted, the reform of the Economic and Monetary Union extended significantly the European Commission's and the Council's competences. The reform brought about three important innovations. First, national budgetary processes were coordinated so that the Commission acquires enough time in order to provide recommendations to member states before national parliaments approve their budgets. Second, the control extended beyond public finances and covered macroeconomic imbalances as well as changes in competitiveness.

Third, the reform introduced stricter procedures for adoption of the Commission's recommendations as well as sanctions for states that have not respected the recommendations. The sanctions concern both financial penalties and restrictions in voting in the Council. In particular, the Commission can impose financial fines up to 0.1 percent of the GDP of a non-compliant state. The fine becomes a non–interest bearing deposit. Furthermore, there is a new decision-making procedure established for the area of European economic governance: the Reverse Qualified Majority Voting Procedure[2] (RQMV). According to the procedure, a Commission's recommendation to impose sanctions on a member state is supposed to be automatically adopted unless the Council decides to reject it by means of the RQMV.

In addition, in order to enhance compliance with the new rules, some member states advocated introduction of the so-called 'balanced budget clause' and 'debt-brake' into national constitutions. Nonetheless, only few EU member states embraced the idea: in most states the fiscal rule has been introduced into the ordinary legislation.

As many economists observed both the initial and the reformed Stability and Growth Pact prioritize strict budgetary consolidation over stabilization policy as the prior goal of the European Semester remains the enforcement of budgetary rigidity (Thygesen, 2013). Given the fact that most EU member states have not had balanced budgets since 2011–2012, it remains questionable whether the standards concerning public finances are likely to meet in the future. Furthermore, it remains open whether the control of macroeconomic imbalances will be executed, particularly with respect to the surplus states.

On one hand, national parliaments' powers in budgetary matters have been further restricted but, on the other, national parliaments acquired new vertical and horizontal avenues to oversight budgetary and economic matters. In particular, the European Semester institutionalized communication between national parliaments and the Commission. Furthermore, through closer coordination of budgetary cycles across the EU member states, national parliaments' awareness of budgetary and economic issues in other states has also increased. As a result, the very practice will tell to what extent national parliaments' activity within the European Semester contributes to the democratic legitimacy of European economic governance.

Notes

1 Regulation 1175/2011, Article 2a.
2 Council Press Release 12/12/2011.

References

Alesina, A. and Rosenthal, H. (1995). *Partisan Politics, Divided Government and the Economy*. Cambridge: Cambridge University Press.

Ardagna, S. (2009). "Financial markets' behaviour around episodes of large changes in the fiscal stance', *European Economic Review*, 53(1), 37–55.

Auel, K. (2007). 'Democratic Accountability and National Parliaments – Re-Defining the Impact of Parliamentary Scrutiny in EU Affairs'. *European Law Journal*, 13(4), 87–504.

Auel, K. and Benz, A. (2005). 'The Politics of Adaptation: Europeanisation of National Parliamentary Systems'. *Journal of Legislative Studies*, 11(3/4), 372–393.

Auel, K. and Christiansen, T. (2015). 'After Lisbon: National Parliaments in the European Union'. *West European Politics*, 38(2), 261–281.

Auel, K. and Hoeing, O. (2014). 'Parliaments in the Euro Crisis: Can the Losers of Integration Still Fight Back?' *Journal of Common Market Studies*, 52(6), 1184–1193.

Auel, K. and Raunio, T. (2014a). 'Introduction: Connecting with the Electorate? Parliamentary Communication in EU Affairs'. *The Journal of Legislative Studies*, 20(1), 1–12, DOI: 10.1080/13572334.2013.871481.

Auel, K. and Raunio, T. (2014b). 'Debating the State of the Union? Comparing Parliamentary Debates on EU Issues in Finland, France, Germany and the United Kingdom'. *The Journal of Legislative Studies*, 20(1), 13–28, DOI: 10.1080/13572334.2013.871482.

Baldacci, E., Gupta, S. and Mulas-Granados, C. (2012). 'How effective is fiscal policy response in financial crises?' available at: http://www.imf.org/external/np/seminars/eng/2012/fincrises/pdf/ch14.pdf.

Baldacci, E., Gupta, S. and Mulas-Granados, C. (2013). 'Debt Reduction, Fiscal Adjustment, and Growth in Credit-Constrained Economies', IMP Working Paper, WP/13/238, URL:https://www.imf.org/external/pubs/ft/wp/2013/wp13238.pdf.

Bardi, L., Bartolini, S. and Trechsel, A. (2014). 'Responsive and Responsible? The Role of Parties in Twenty-First Century Politics'. *West European Politics*, 37(2), 235–252, DOI: 10.1080/01402382.2014.887871.

Begg, I. (2013). 'The Cypriot Banking Crisis Shows That Europeans Have Yet to Work Out the Answer to the Question, "Who Pays?"'. *LSE Blog*, Retrieved from:

http://blogs.lse.ac.uk/europpblog/2013/03/26/the-cypriot-banking-crisis-shows-that-europeans-have-yet-to-work-out-the-answer-to-the-question-who-pays/.

Benz, A. (2013). 'An Asymmetric Two-Level Game: Parliaments in the Euro Crisis', in: Crum, B. and Fossum, J. E. (eds) *Practices of Inter-Parliamentary Coordination in International Politics: The European Union and Beyond.* Colchester: ECPR Press, pp. 156–176.

Bergman, T. (1997). 'National Parliaments and EU Affairs Committees: Notes on Empirical Variation and Competing Explanations'. *Journal of European Public Policy*, 4(3), 373–387.

Birch, A. H. (1964). *Representative and Responsive Government.* London: George Allen & Unwin.

Blondel, J. (1973). *Comparative Legislatures.* Upper Saddle River, NJ: Prentice-Hall.

Bohle, D. (2014). 'Responsible Government and Capitalism's Cycles'. *West European Politics*, 37(2), 288–308, DOI: 10.1080/01402382.2014.887876.

Boix, C. (2000). 'Partisan Governments, the International Economy, and Macroeconomic Policies in Advanced Nations, 1960–93'. *World Politics*, 53, 38–73.

Born, H. and Hänggi, H. (Eds.) (2004). *The Double Democratic Deficit: Parliamentary Accountability and the Use of Force under International Auspices* (pp. 53–72). Aldershot: Ashgate.

Born, H., Dowling, A., Fuior, T. and Gavrilescu, S. (2007). *Parliamentary Oversight of Civilian and Military ESDP Missions: The European and National Levels.* Brussels: European Parliament.

Born, H. and Hänggi, H. (2005). 'The Use of Force under International Auspices Strengthening Parliamentary Accountability'. DCAF Policy Paper, No. 7, Geneva: Centre for the Democratic Control of Armed Forces.

Borz, G. and Rose, R. (2013). 'Aggregation and Representation in European Parliamentary Party Groups'. *West European Politics*, 36(3), 474–497.

Broz, L. (2013). 'Partisan Financial Cycles', in: Lake D. L. and Kahler M. (eds) *Politics in the New Hard Times: The Great Recession in Comparative Perspective.* Ithaca, NY: Cornell University Press.

Buehn, A. and Schneider, F. (2011). 'Shadow Economies around the World: Novel Insights, Accepted Knowledge and New Estimates'. *International Tax and Public Finance*, 19, 139–171.

Burke, E. (1774/1854). 'Speech to the Electors of Bristol', in: Bohn, H. G. (ed) *The Works of the Right Honorable Edmund Burke*, 446–48. London: H. G. Bohn.

Buti, M. and Pench, L. R. (2004). 'Why Do Large Countries Flout the Stability Pact? And What Can Be Done About It?' *Journal of Common Market Studies*, 42(5), 1025–1032.

Campbell, J. L. (2010). 'Neoliberalism In Crisis: Regulatory Roots of the U.S. Financial Meltdown', in: Lounsbury, M. and Hirsch, P. M. (eds) *Markets on Trial: The Economic Sociology of the U.S. Financial Crisis.* Emerald Group Publishing Limited. Bingley.

Cartabia, M., Lamarque, E. and Tanzarella, P. (Eds.) (2011). *Gli atti normativi del Governo tra Corte costituzionale e giudici.* Giappichelli: Torino.

Closa, C. and Maatsch, A. (2014). 'In a Spirit of Solidarity? Justifying the European Financial Stability Facility (EFSF) in National Parliamentary Debates'. *Journal of Common Market Studies*, 52(4), 826–842.

Cooper, I. (2014). 'Parliamentary Oversight of the EU after the Crisis: On the Creation of the 'Article 13' Interparliamentary Conference'. LUISS Guido Carli School of Government Working Paper No. SOG-WP21/2014. Retrieved from: http://dx.doi.org/10.2139/ssrn.2488723.

Cottarelli, C. and Jaramillo, L. (2012). 'Walking Hand in Hand: Fiscal Policy and Growth in Advanced Economies', IMF Working Paper No. 12/137, available at: http://papers.ssrn.com/sol3/papers.cfm?abstract_id=2127031.

Coutts, S., Díez Sánchez, L., Marketou, A. and Pierdominici, L. (2015). 'Legal Manifestations of the Emergency in National Euro Crisis Law'. EUI Working Papers, LAW 2015/14, Retrieved from: http://cadmus.eui.eu/bitstream/han dle/1814/35499/LAW_2015_14.pdf?sequence=1.

Cranston, M. W. and Mair, P. (1980). *Ideology and Politics*. Berlin: Springer.

Crespy, A. and Gajewska, K. (2010). 'New Parliament, New Cleavages after the Eastern Enlargement? The Conflict over the Services Directive as an Opposition between the Liberals and the Regulators. *Journal of Common Market Studies*, 48(5), 1185–1208.

Crespy, A. and Schmidt, V. (2014). 'The Clash of Titans: France, Germany and the Discursive Double Game of EMU Reform'. *Journal of European Public Policy*, 21(8), 1085–1101.

Crum, B. (2013). 'Saving the Euro at the Cost of Democracy?' *Journal of Common Market Studies*, 51(4), 614–630.

Dalton, R. (1985). 'Political Parties and Political Representation: Party Supporters and Party Elites in Nine Nations'. *Comparative Political Studies*, 17(3), 267–299.

Dawson, M. and de Witte, F. (2013). 'Constitutional Balance in the EU after the Euro-Crisis'. *The Modern Law Review*, 76, 817–844, DOI: 10.1111/1468-2230.12037.

De Giorgi, E. and Moury, C. (2015). 'Conclusions: Great Recession, Great Cooperation?' *The Journal of Legislative Studies*, 21(1), 115–120, DOI: 10.1080/13572334.2014.939560.

De Grauwe, P. and Ji, Y. (2012). 'Mispricing of Sovereign Risk and Macroeconomic Stability in the Eurozone'. *Journal of Common Market Studies*, 50, 866–880.

De Ruiter, R. (2013). 'Under the Radar? National Parliaments and the Ordinary Legislative Procedure in the European Union'. *Journal of European Public Policy*, 20(8), 1196–1212.

de Vreese, C. H. and Kandyla, A. (2009). 'News Framing and Public Support for a Common Foreign and Security Policy'. *Journal of Common Market Studies*, 47(3), 453–482.

De Wilde, P. (2010). *How Politicisation Affects European Integration: Contesting the EU Budget in the Netherlands, Denmark and Ireland*. PhD Dissertation, Oslo: Unipub.

De Witte, B. (2011). 'The European Treaty Amendment for the Creation of a Financial Stability Mechanism'. SIEPS European Policy Analysis. Retrieved from: http://www.sieps.se/sites/default/files/2011_6epa.pdf.

De Witte, B., Trechsel, A.H., Damjanović, D., Hellquist, E. and Ponzano, P. (2010). 'Legislating after Lisbon: New Opportunities for the European Parliament'. A study prepared in the framework of the European Union Democracy Observatory (EUDO), under the direction of Professor Alexander H.

Trechsel and Professor Bruno de Witte. Retrieved from: https://www.eui.eu/Projects/EUDO-LegislatingafterLisbon(SD).pdf.

Dell'Anno, R., Gomez-Antonio, M. and Alañon-Pardo, A. (2007). 'The Underground Economy in Three Mediterranean Countries: France, Spain and Greece – A MIMIC Approach'. *Empirical Economics*, 33, 51–84.

Downs, A. (1957). *An Economic Theory of Democracy*, New York: Harper.

Duina, F. and Oliver, M. 2005. 'National Parliaments in the European Union: Are There Any Benefits to Integration?' *European Law Journal*, 11(2), 173–195.

Dyson, K. (2000). 'EMU as Europeanization: Convergence, Diversity and Contingency'. *Journal of Common Market Studies*, 38(4), 645–666.

Dyson, K. and Featherstone, K. (1999). *The Road to Maastricht: Negotiating Economic and Monetary Union*. Oxford: Oxford University Press.

Enderlein, H. and Verdun, A. (2009). 'EMU's Teenage Challenge: What Have We Learned and What Can We Predict from Political Science?' *Journal of European Public Policy*, 16(4), 490–507.

Ezrow, L., De Vries, C., Steenberger, M. and Edwards, E. (2010). 'Mean Voter Representation and Partisan Constituency Representation: Do Parties Respond to the Mean Voter Position or to Their Supporters?' *Party Politics*, 17(3), 275–301.

Fasone, C. (2014a). 'National Parliaments under External Fiscal Constraints. The Case of Italy, Portugal and Spain Facing the Eurozone Crisis'. Working Paper Series, SOG-WP19/2014 ISSN: 2282–4189.

Fasone, C. (2014b). 'European Economic Governance and Parliamentary Representation: What Place for the European Parliament?' *European Law Journal*, 20(2), 164–185.

Fasone, C. (2014c). 'Eurozone, Non-Eurozone and "Troubled Asymmetries" among National Parliaments in the EU. Why and to What Extent This Is of Concern'. *Perspectives on Federalism*, 6(3), 1–41.

Fasone, C. (2015). 'Taking Budgetary Powers Away from National Parliaments? On Parliamentary Prerogatives in the Eurozone Crisis'. EUI Working Papers, LAW 2015/37.

Featherstone, K. (2011). 'The Greek Sovereign Debt Crisis and EMU: A Failing State in a Skewed Regime'. *Journal of Common Market Studies*, 49(2), 193–217.

Foret, F. and Rittelmeyer, Y.S. (eds.) (2015). *The European Council and European Governance*. The commanding heights of the EU. London: Routledge.

Furceri, D. and Sousa, R.M. (2009). 'The impact of government spending on the private sector: crowding-out versus crowding-in effects', online paper available at: http://www.eeg.uminho.pt/economia/nipe.

Galella, P. and Maatsch, A. (2016). 'Parliamentary Oversight of European Security Policy: A Matter of Formal Competences or the Will of Parliamentarians?' (PADEMIA Online Papers on Parliamentary Democracy).

Gamson, W.A. and Modigliani, A. (1989). 'Media Discourse and Public Opinion on Nuclear Power: A Constructionist Approach'. *American Journal of Sociology*, 95, 1–37.

Gitlin, T. (1980). *The Whole World Is Watching*. Berkeley: University of California Press.

Goffman, I. (1974). *Frame Analysis: An Essay on the Organization of Experience*. London: Harper and Row.

Goffman, I. (1981). *Forms of Talk*. Philadelphia: University of Pennsylvania Press.

Habermas, J. (1991). 'Vom pragmatischen, ethischen und moralischen Gebrauch der praktischen Vernunft', in: Habermas, J. (ed) *Erläuterungen zur Diskursethik*. Frankfurt/Main: Suhrkamp, pp. 100–118.

Haede, U. (2009). 'Haushaltsdisziplin und Solidarität im Zeichen der Finanzkrise'. *Europäische Zeitschrift für Wirtschaftsrecht*, 12, 399–423.

Hall, P. (2014). 'Varieties of Capitalism and the Euro Crisis'. *West European Politics*, 37(6), 1223–1243.

Hefftler, C., Kreilinger, V., Rosenberg, O. and Wessels, W. (2013). 'National Parliaments: Their Emerging Control Over the European Council'. Policy Paper, Notre Europe, Jacques Delors Institute.

Hefftler, C., Neuhold, C., Rozenberg, O. and Smith, J. (2015). *The Palgrave Handbook of National Parliaments and the European Union*. Basingstoke: Palgrave Macmillan.

Heipertz, M. and Verdun, A. (2005). 'The Stability and Growth Pact – Theorizing a Case in European Integration'. *Journal of Common Market Studies*, 43(5), 985–1008.

Hibbing, J. R. and Theiss-Morse, E. (2001). 'Process Preferences and American Politics: What the People Want Government to Be'. *The American Political Science Review*, 95(1), 145–153. Stable Retrieved from: http://links.jstor.org/sici?sici=0003-0554%28200103%2995%3A1%3C145%3APPAAPW%3E2.0.CO%3B2-3.

Hix, S. and Noury, A. (2009). 'After Enlargement: Voting Patterns in the Sixth European Parliament'. *Legislative Studies Quarterly*, 34(2), 159–174.

Hooghe, L. and Marks, G. (2008). 'A Postfunctionalist Theory of European Integration: From Permissive Consensus to Constraining Dissensus'. *British Journal of Political Science*, 39, 1–23.

Jabko, N. (2011). 'Which Economic Governance for the European Union? Facing Up the Problem of Divided Sovereignty'. Swedish Institute for European Policy Studies, Report No.2, March 2011. Retrieved from: www.sieps.se.

Jančić, D. (2016). National Parliaments and EU Fiscal Integration, *European Law Journal*, vol. 22(2), 225–249.

Judge, D. (1995). 'The Failure of National Parliaments'. *West European Politics*, 18(3), 79–100.

Jullien, B. and Smith, A. (2016). *The EU's Government of Industries*. Markets, Institutions and Politics. London: Routledge.

Kaczyński, P. M. (2011). 'Paper Tigers or Sleeping Beauties? National Parliaments in the Post-Lisbon European Political System'. CEPS Special Reports, February 2011. Retrieved from: http://www.ceps.eu/node/4144.

Kröger, S. and Bellamy, R. (2016). 'Beyond Constraining Dissensus? The Role of National Parliaments in Politicizing European Integration'. *Comparative European Politics*, 14(2), 131–153.

Krugman, P. (2012). *End This Depression Now!* New York: W. W. Norton & Company.

Kumar, M.S. and Woo, J. (2010). 'Public Debt and Growth', IMF Working Paper, available at: http://www.imf.org/external/pubs/cat/longres.cfm?sk=24080.0.

References

Lord, C. (2012). 'On Legitimacy of Monetary Union'. SIEPS Report 2012:3.

Louis, J. V. (2010). 'The No Bailout Clause and Rescue Packages'. *Common Market Law Review*, 47(4), 971–986.

Lupato, F. G. (2014). 'Talking Europe, Using Europe: The EU and Parliamentary Competition in Italy and Spain (1986–2006)'. *The Journal of Legislative Studies*, 20(1), 29–45, DOI: 10.1080/13572334.2013.871483.

Maatsch, A. (2010). 'Between an Intergovernmental and a Polycentric European Union: National Parliamentary Discourses on Democracy in the EU Ratification Process'. RECON online papers, 2010/18.

Maatsch, A. (2013). 'Watch-Dogs That Cannot Bite? New National Parliamentary Control Mechanisms under the Lisbon Treaty', in: Liebert, U. (ed) *Democratizing the EU from Below? Citizenship, Civil Society and the Public Sphere*. New York: Ashgate, 1315–1356.

Maatsch, A. (2014). 'Are We All Austerians Now? An Analysis of National Parliamentary Parties' Positioning on Anti-Crisis Measures in the Eurozone'. *Journal of European Public Policy*, 21(1), 96–115, DOI: 10.1080/13501763.2013.829582.

Maatsch, A. (2015). 'Limited and Asymmetrical: Approval of Anti-Crisis Measures by National Parliaments in the Eurozone', in: Fasone, C., Fromage, D. and Lefkofridi, Z. (eds) *Parliaments, Public Opinion and Parliamentary Elections in Europe* (EUI Working Papers Series).

Maatsch, A. (2016). 'Drivers of Political Parties' Voting Behaviour in European Economic Governance: The Ultimate Decline of the Economic Cleavage?' in: *West European Politics*, 39(4). DOI: 10.1080/01402382.2015.1129491.

Maatsch, A. (2017). 'European Semester Compliance and National Political Party Ownership', in Jančić, D. National Parliaments after the Lisbon Treaty and the Euro Crisis (Oxford: Oxford University Press).

Maduro, M. (2012). 'A New Governance for the European Union and the Euro: Democracy and Justice'. EUI RSCAS Policy Paper, RSCAS PP 2012/11, European University Institute. Retrieved from: http://cadmus.eui.eu/bitstream/handle/1814/24295/RSCAS_PP_2012_11rev.pdf?sequence=1.

Mair, P. (2009). 'Representative Versus Responsible Government'. MPIfG Working Paper 09/8, Cologne. Retrieved from: http://www.mpifg.de/pu/workpap/wp09-8.pdf.

Mair, P. (2011). 'Bini Smaghi vs. The Parties: Representative Government and Institutional Constraints'. EUI Working Papers, RSCAS 2011/22, Retrieved from: http://cadmus.eui.eu/bitstream/handle/1814/16354/RSCAS_2011_22.pdf? . . . 1.

Mankiw, N. G. and Romer, D. (1991). *New Keynesian Economics – Vol. 1: Imperfect Competition and Sticky Prices*, Cambridge: MA MIT Press.

Maurer, A. and Wessels, W. (2001). *National Parliaments on Their Ways to Europe: Losers or Latecomers?* Baden-Baden: Nomos.

Mayoral, J. (2011). 'Democratic Improvements in the European Union under the Lisbon Treaty. Insitutional Changes Regarding Democratic Government in the EU'. EUDO Report. Retrieved from: https://www.eui.eu/Projects/EUDO-Institutions/Documents/EUDOreport922011.pdf.

McNamara, K. (1999). *The Currency of Ideas: Monetary Politics in the European Union*. Ithaca, NY: Cornell University Press.

Norton, P. (1995). 'Conclusion: Addressing the Democratic Deficit'. *Journal of Legislative Studies*, 1(3), 177–193.

Norman, L. (2016). *The Mechanism of Institutional Conflict in the European Union*. London: Routledge.

O'Brennan, J. and Raunio, T. (2007). *National Parliaments within the Enlarged European Union: From Victims of Integration to Competitive Actors?* Oxon: Routledge.

Pernice, I. (2014). 'Domestic Courts, Constitutional Constraints and European Democracy: What Solution for the Crisis?' in: Adams, M., Fabbrini, F. and Larouche, P. (eds) *The Constitutionalisation of European Budgetary Constraints*. Oxford: Hart Publishing, 297–319.

Pollak, J. and Slominski, P. (2014). 'The Silence of the Shepherds: How the Austrian Parliament Informs Its Citizens on European Issues'. *The Journal of Legislative Studies*, 20(1), 109–124, DOI: 10.1080/13572334.2013.871488.

Puetter, U. (2012). 'Europe's Deliberative Intergovernmentalism: The Role of the Council and European Council in EU Economic Governance'. *Journal of European Public Policy*, 19(2), 161–178.

Ragin, C.C. (1987). *The Comparative Method: Moving Beyond Qualitative and Quantitative Strategies*, Berkley: University of California Press.

Raunio, T. (2009). 'National Parliaments and European Integration: What We Know and Agenda for Future Research'. *The Journal of Legislative Studies*, 15(4), 317–334.

Raunio, T. and Hix, S. (2000). 'Backbenchers Learn to Fight Back: European Integration and Parliamentary Government'. *West European Politics*, 23(4), 142–168.

Rihoux, B. and Ragin, C. (eds.) (2009). *Configurational Comparative Methods. Qualitative Comparative Analysis (QCA) and Related Techniques, Applied Social Research Methods*, Thousand Oaks and London: Sage.

Risse, T. (2014). 'No Demos? Identities and Public Spheres in the Euro Crisis'. *JCMS: Journal of Common Market Studies*, 52, 1207–1215, DOI: 10.1111/jcms.12189.

Rittberger, B. (2014). 'Integration without Representation? The European Parliament and the Reform of Economic Governance in the EU'. *Journal of Common Market Studies*, 52(6), 1174–1183.

Rodrik, D. (2011). *The Globalization Paradox: Democracy and the Future of the World Economy*. New York: W. W. Norton.

Rose, R. (2014). 'Responsible Party Government in a World of Interdependence'. *West European Politics*, 37(2), 253–269, DOI: 10.1080/01402382.2014.887874.

Ruffert, M. (2011). 'The European Debt Crisis and European Union Law'. *Common Market Law Review*, 48, 1777–1806.

Saalfeld, T. (2005). 'Deliberate Delegation or Abdication? Government Backbenchers, Ministers and European Union Legislation'. *The Journal of Legislative Studies*, 11, 343–371.

Scharpf, F. (2009). 'Legitimacy in the Multilevel European Polity'. *European Political Science Review*, 1, 173–204, DOI: 10.1017/S1755773909000204.

Scharpf, F. (2014). 'After the Crash: A Perspective on Multilevel European Democracy'. MPIfG Discussion Paper 14/21. Retrieved from: http://www.mpifg.de/pu/mpifg_dp/dp14–21.pdf.

Schmidt, V. (2011). 'The Problems of Identity and Legitimacy in the European Union', in: Lucarelli, S., Cerutti, F. and Schmidt, V. (eds) *Debating Political Identity and Legitimacy in the European Union*. London: Routledge/Garnet Series: Europe in the World, 16–38.

Schneider, C.Q. and Wagemann, C. (2007). Qualitative Comparative Analysis (QCA) und Fuzzy Sets. *Ein Lehrbuch fuer Anwender und jende, die es werden wollen*, Opladen: Barbara Budrich.

Seyad, S.M. (2010). 'A Legal Analysis of the European Financial Stability Mechanism'. *Journal of International Banking Law and Regulation*, 26(9), 421–433.

Szczerbiak, A. and Taggart, P. (2008). *Opposing Europe? The Comparative Party Politics of Euroscepticism. Volume 1: Case Studies and Country Surveys*. Oxford: Oxford University Press.

Szczerbiak, A. and Taggart, P. (2013). 'Coming in from the Cold? Euroscepticism, Government Participation and Party Positions on Europe'. *JCMS: Journal of Common Market Studies*, 51, 17–37.

Tannen, D. (1993). *Framing in Discourse*. Oxford: Oxford University Press.

Thompson, H. (2013). 'The Crisis of the Euro: The Problem of German Power Revisited'. SPERI Paper No. 8, Sheffield Political Economy Research Institute, Retrieved from: http://speri.dept.shef.ac.uk/wp-content/uploads/2013/01/SPERI-Paper-NO.8-The-Crisisof-the-Euro-The-Problem-of-German-Power-Revisited-PDF-536KB.pdf.

Thygesen, N. (2013). "Governance in the Euro Area: Approaching an Optimum Currency Area?" in: Verdun, A. and Tovias, A. (Eds.) *Mapping Economic Integration* (London: Palgrave Macmillan).

Townsend, M. (2006). *The Euro and the Monetary Union: An Historical, Institutional and Economic Description*. London: John Harper Publishing.

Trenz, H.J. and Michailidou, M. (2013). 'Mediated Representative Politics in the European Union: Towards Audience Democracy?' *Journal of European Public Policy*, 20(2), 260–277.

van Dijk, T.A. and Wodak, R. (2000). *Racism at the Top. Parliamentary Discourse on Ethnic Issues in Six European States*. Klagenfurt: Drava Verlag.

Weiler, J. (1999). *The Constitution of Europe*. Cambridge: Cambridge University Press.

Wendel, M. (2013). 'Judicial Restraint and the Return to Openness: The Decision of the German Federal Constitutional Court on the ESM and the Fiscal Treaty of 12 September 2012'. *German Law Journal*, 14, 21–32.

Wendler, F. (2011). 'Die Politisierung der europäischen Integration: Nationale Parlamentsdebatten zur Europäischen Union im Bundestag und House of Commons'. *Zeitschrift für Parlamentsfragen*, 2, 307–325.

Wendler, F. (2014). 'Justification and Political Polarization in National Parliamentary Debates on EU Treaty Reform'. *Journal of European Public Policy*, 21(4), 549–567, DOI: 10.1080/13501763.2014.882388.

Index

Note: Page numbers in *italics* indicate tables.

accountability 11–14
Amsterdam Treaty 5
anti-austerian groups 82–4, 86
anti-crisis measures: approvals of *38–41*, 109–11; database 37; dependent variable 42; discourses of parliamentary parties 75–6; discursive support and opposition 78–80, *79*; economic stance of parties and 89–90; voting behaviour of political parties 56–63, 68–70, *71–2*, 73; *see also* emergency legislation; European Financial Stability Facility; European Stability Mechanism; Treaty on Stability, Coordination and Governance in the Economic and Monetary Union
Article 10, Treaty on European Union 8
Article 12, Treaty on European Union 8–9
austerity policies 61, 91–2

bailout states: acceleration of legislative process in 111; budgetary plans of 52; Cyprus 30; 'double positioning' of parties in 103–4; Eurosceptic parties in 62; Fiscal Compact and 53; Greece 26; Ireland 27; loss of substantive equality of 111; macroeconomic preferences of 94–5, 104, 105–6; parliamentary democracy in 116; parliamentary party voting behaviour in 63; political discourse of 90; political parties in 57; Portugal 29; voters in 13
Burke, Edmund 1

common currency zone 22–3, 56, 60, 95, 115
communication of national parliaments 74–5; *see also* discourses of parliamentary parties
Conference of Parliamentary Committees for Union Affairs 5–6
constitutional set-up and application of emergency legislation 49–50
control function of national parliaments 111–15
courts, national, and application of emergency legislation 49–52, 111
creditor states: approval of anti-crisis measures by 46–7; Eurosceptic parties in 62; macroeconomic preferences of 94–5, 104, 105–6; parliamentary party voting behaviour in 63; political discourse of 90; political parties in 57–8
Cyprus, financial crisis in 29–30

debtor states 52; *see also* bailout states
decision-making in EU: democratization of 10–11; legitimacy of 2
de-parliamentarization in EU 4, 6
devaluation and trade deficits 28

discourses of parliamentary parties: analytical framework 76–7, 96–9; methodological approach 77–8; nationalist and anti-austerian opponents 82–4; overview 74–6, 85–7, 113–14; pragmatic and idealistic supporters 80–1; support and opposition, dominant frames of 78–80, 79

disempowerment of southern European parliaments 37, 51, 53–4, 63, 110

disempowerment thesis 43–4, 86

Early Warning System 9

Economic and Monetary Union: institutional weakness of 22; reform process of 2, 118–19

economic governance *see* reform of economic governance

economic interdependence in eurozone 60, 94

EFSF *see* European Financial Stability Facility

emergency legislation: approval of 109–11; conceptualization of 45–6; defined 36; as dependent variable of study 42; European financial crisis and 46–9; factors influencing application of 49–53; implementation of 44–5; *see also* anti-crisis measures

equality of national representative institutions 54–5, 111

ESM *see* European Stability Mechanism

ethical discourses/frames 76–8, 81, 85

European Central Bank 52

European Commission 52

European Economic Recovery Plan 24

European financial crisis: application of emergency legislation during 46–9; legal status of anti-crisis measures 30–3; legitimacy gap and 13; overview 22–30; *see also* anti-crisis measures

European Financial Stability Facility (EFSF): establishment and approval of 47; German Constitutional Court ruling on 50; legal status of 30–1; plenary parliamentary debates on 97; purpose of 42; Spain and 27

European integration process: discourses of parliamentary parties on 86; input legitimacy and 12; national parliament adaptations to 4–8; reform of 13–14; support for, and party voting behaviour 67, 69, 70

European Parliament: democratic accountability of 54; institutional limitations of 12; powers of, after Lisbon Treaty 9–11

European Semester 117–20

European Stability Mechanism (ESM): German Constitutional Court ruling on 50; legal status of 30, 31, 32; purpose of 42; treaty establishing 47–8

European Union (EU): decision-making in 2, 10–11; de-parliamentarization in 4, 6; international trade and 9–10; normalization of politics of 14, 70, 73; re-parliamentarization in 4–8; *see also specific treaties*

Eurosceptic opposition parties 62, 69, 82–4, 86

fast-track procedures 36, 44, 109–11; *see also* emergency legislation

Fiscal Compact 31–2; *see also* Treaty on Stability, Coordination and Governance in the Economic and Monetary Union

frames and frame analysis 77–8

free trade agreements 9–10

functions of parliaments 2–3, 42, 74, 111–15; *see also* oversight, parliamentary

Germany: empowerment of parliament in 50–1; financial crisis in 28

global financial crisis 23; *see also* European financial crisis

governing parties: economic stance of 90, 104; ethical arguments of 81; macroeconomic preferences of 93–4; pragmatic arguments of 80–1, 85; voting behaviour of 59–60, 66, 69

Index 131

Greece: financial crisis in 24, 25–6; plenary debates to Fiscal Compact in 84

ideology of political parties 61–2, 93, 104
input legitimacy 11–12, 13, 57
International Monetary Fund 52
international obligations, responsibility towards 59–60, 69, 113
international trade and EU 9–10
Interparliamentary Conference on Stability, Economic Coordination and Governance 55
Ireland, financial crisis in 26–7

Keynesianism 90, 91–2, 99, *101*, 101–2, *102*

legal status of anti-crisis measures 30–3
legislative mergers 36, 46, 48–9, 84, 110
legitimacy: of decision-making in EU 2; input and output 11–12, 13, 57; of political systems 57
legitimacy gap 6, 11–14

Macroeconomic Imbalance Procedure 33
macroeconomic preferences of parliamentary parties: codes in OCA model *95*; discourse analysis of plenary debates 96–9; 'double' positioned parties 103–4; empirical findings *101*, 101–6, *102*, *103*; factors in 92–6; Keynesianism and neoliberalism 91–2; methodological approach 91, 96–100; overview 89–91, 106–7, 114–15; positioned parties *101*, 101–2, *102*, *103*; QCA crisp-set analysis 99–100
Memoranda of Understanding and bailout loans 52, 97
mergers, legislative 36, 46, 48–9, 84, 110
moral arguments/frames 76–7, 78

'nationalist' groups 82, 86
neoliberalism 23, 90, 91–2, 98–9, 102, *103*

Nice Treaty 11
normalization of EU politics 14, 70, 73
northern European parliaments, empowerment of 54

opposition parties: discourse on anti-crisis measures of 81–4; idealistic arguments of 85; macroeconomic preferences of 93–4; 'salience' of 106; voting behaviour of 59, 60–2, 66–7, 69–70
ordinary legislative procedure 11
output legitimacy 11, 13, 57
oversight, parliamentary: emergency legislation and 49–53; of European economic governance 14; factors in 7; inequality of 54–5; role of, in policy-making 42–5

Papandreou, George 25–6
parliamentary parties: assessment of performance of 116–17; functions of 56–7; information deficits of 86–7; *see also* discourses of parliamentary parties; governing parties; macroeconomic preferences of parliamentary parties; opposition parties; voting behaviour of political parties
parliaments, national: analysis of activities of 108–9; approval of anti-crisis measures by 109–11; communication of 74–5; from de-parliamentarization to re-parliamentarization 4–8; disempowerment of 53–4, 86; emergency legislation as limiting powers of 46; within European Semester 117–20; functions of 2–3, 42, 74, 111–15; inequality of 111; legitimacy gap and 6, 11–14; power asymmetries in 37, 110; power of 108, 115–17; re-empowerment of 54; in reform of European economic governance 1–4; role of, after Lisbon Treaty 8–11; *see also* European Parliament; oversight, parliamentary; southern European parliaments, disempowerment of

PIREDEU database 64, 65–6
plenary debates *see* discourses of parliamentary parties
Portugal, financial crisis in 28–9
pragmatic discourses/frames 76–7, 80–1, 85

Qualified Majority Vote 4, 12
Qualitative Comparative Analysis (QCA) crisp-set analysis 99–100

re-empowerment of parliaments 54
reform of economic governance: application of emergency legislation during 49–53; assessment of performance during 116–17; drivers of political party behaviour in 58–63, 66–8, *67*; parliaments in 1–4; redistribution, choice of strategies, and 89; voting behaviour of political parties 56–63
Regulation 472/2013 33
Regulation 473/2013 33
re-parliamentarization in EU 4–8
representative democracy, principle of 1, 13
representative function of national parliaments 111–15
republican intergovernmentalism 13–14
responsibility of political parties 57, 59–60, 69, 112, 115, 116
responsiveness of political parties 56–7, 60–1, 69–70, 112, 113, 116
Reverse Qualified Majority Voting Procedure 119

shadow banking system 23–4
southern European parliaments, disempowerment of 37, 51, 53–4, 63, 110
sovereign debt crisis *see* European financial crisis
Spain: approval of anti-crisis measures in 51; financial crisis in 24, 27–8
Stability and Growth Pact 22, 24, 31, 119
support for anti-crisis measures 80–1

Treaty of Lisbon 5–6, 8–11
Treaty of Maastricht 5
Treaty on European Union 8–9, 11
Treaty on Stability, Coordination and Governance in the Economic and Monetary Union: German Constitutional Court ruling on 50; legal status of 31–2; plenary debates on in Greece 84; purpose of 42; ratification procedures 48, 53, 110
Treaty on the Functioning of the European Union 9–10
'Troika' 52

United States, financial crisis in 23–4

voting behaviour of parliamentarians, asymmetry with discourses 79
voting behaviour of political parties: on anti-crisis measures 59–63; empirical findings on 66–70, *67*, *71–2*, 73; overview 56–9; representation and 112; study of 63–6